# MACARTHUR

## The Supreme Commander at War in the Pacific

James W. Zobel

STACKPOLE
BOOKS

Copyright © 2015 by James W. Zobel

Published by
STACKPOLE BOOKS
5067 Ritter Road
Mechanicsburg, PA 17055
www.stackpolebooks.com

Printed in the United States of America

10  9  8  7  6  5  4  3  2  1

*Cover design by Caroline Stover*

**Library of Congress Cataloging-in-Publication Data**

Zobel, James W.
   MacArthur : the Supreme Commander at war in the Pacific / James W. Zobel. — First edition.
      pages cm. — (Stackpole military photo series)
   Includes bibliographical references.
   ISBN 978-0-8117-1547-8
1.  MacArthur, Douglas, 1880–1964.  2.  World War, 1939–1945—Campaigns—Pacific Area.  3.  Generals—United States—Biography.  4.  United States. Army—Officers—Biography.  5.  Pacific Area—History, Military.  I. Title.
   D767.Z63 2014
   940.54'1273092—dc23
      [B]                                        2014043691

# CONTENTS

# INTRODUCTION

Gen. Douglas MacArthur had a full military career of accolades and disappointments. The son of a famous general who was a hero of the American Civil War, Douglas did his best to emulate his father on the fields of France in the First World War. He emerged from that conflict as one of the youngest general officers in the United States Army and as one of the most highly decorated Americans. MacArthur reached the pinnacle of his career in 1930 as Chief of Staff of the United States Army, the highest position an army officer can reach. He was the youngest ever to do so. In 1935 he moved to the Philippines and retired from the army in 1937. His career was over—or at least he thought it was.

The Empire of Japan created the need for Douglas MacArthur to become a soldier again. Japan's wars in Asia threatened the national interests of the United States, and the Philippines were in the direct path of Japan's ambitions. MacArthur was recalled to active duty and given command in the Philippines: a command that most in the U.S. military believed would be sacrificed at the outset of war. MacArthur exuded confidence, but that never outweighs material might. The Japanese attacked in December 1941, and like at Pearl Harbor, MacArthur tasted disaster at the outset. He made brilliant moves and mistakes after the Japanese invasion, but was ordered away from his command to Australia before the end came: the worst defeat in American history. Whereas the commanders at Pearl Harbor saw their careers terminated, MacArthur was given another chance.

Arriving in Australia, MacArthur found he had nothing with which to take the offensive against the Japanese, and the geography of the Pacific presented a major problem. War in the Pacific was nothing like what he had witnessed in France in the First World War. Air power was dominant, something he had to learn. There were no roads to Tokyo and victory. The highway of the Pacific was water. MacArthur had to become a master of combined arms—air, land, and sea—to prosecute this war. He handpicked a team of generals and admirals to help him and won the confidence of the Allied Powers to give him the support he needed to wage war.

Throughout the Second World War, MacArthur was last on a long list of those who needed men and supplies to win the war. Many in the U.S. War Department never thought he would leave Australia because he wasn't being given anything to fight with, but in conjunction with U.S. naval forces, MacArthur and his Australian allies went on the offensive in the Pacific in late 1942. MacArthur's drive was always on the verge of being shut down for a concentrated push by naval forces in the Central Pacific. It was his string of unbroken victories that kept it alive.

Allied strategy was focused on the defeat of Japan by the quickest possible method. MacArthur was too, but his method was always through the Philippines. Defeat in the Philippines was forever on his mind, and the only way to erase that stain on his career and taste redemption was to return and liberate the islands. It was a quest not shared by the Navy, the War Department, or the Allied Powers. Circumstances, opportunity, and the will of Douglas MacArthur convinced them otherwise, and he was able fulfill his famous promise and the quote he will forever be remembered for: "I shall return."

To his contemporaries, MacArthur was proud and, many thought, egotistical, but they also saw his brilliance; that was why he was given another chance after defeat in the Philippines. They knew he could contribute to ultimate victory over Japan. He proved them right. Had the Second World War never occurred, MacArthur would be a footnote in American history, maybe worth a line or two in the history books. MacArthur, however, was never a man for the periphery, and the Second World War made him a household name, revealing all his greatness and flaws.

Douglas MacArthur was the grandson of Arthur MacArthur, an immigrant from Scotland who came to the United States at age ten with his mother, Sarah. Arthur grew up in Massachusetts, studied law, married, and made a life as a lawyer, a lieutenant governor of Wisconsin, and a judge. He had two sons, Arthur Jr. and Frank. He was a man who would use his wit and political connections to further the careers of his sons and grandsons.

Arthur MacArthur Jr. was the "boy colonel" of the Union Army in the American Civil War. When Arthur was seventeen, his father obtained him a position as regimental adjutant of the 24th Wisconsin Infantry. His character and bearing earned respect, and by war's end he held the rank of colonel and commanded the regiment. His bravery at Missionary Ridge in November 1863 qualified him for the Medal of Honor. Arthur MacArthur Jr. was the dominant influence on Douglas MacArthur's life.

After a brief stint trying to be a lawyer, Arthur MacArthur Jr. chose the life of a soldier. He was quickly promoted to captain in the Regular Army and wore the rank for twenty-six years. His early postwar career entailed occupation duty in the defeated Confederacy. In 1870 he was serving in New Orleans, Louisiana, with the 13th Infantry (front row, second from right). It was there he met Mary Hardy.

Mary Pinkney Hardy was the daughter of a cotton broker and merchant from Norfolk, Virginia. Well-educated, she was on vacation in New Orleans when she met Captain MacArthur. Five years later they were married at her home in Norfolk; her Confederate brothers refused to attend the wedding. She bore three sons to Captain MacArthur: Arthur in 1876, Malcolm in 1878, and Douglas in 1880.

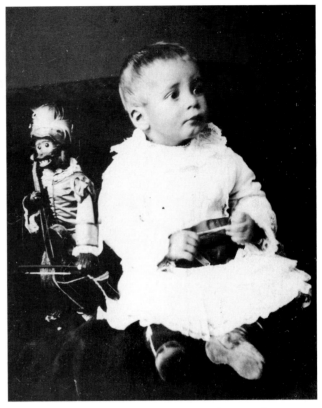

On January 26, 1880, Douglas MacArthur was born at the Arsenal Barracks in Little Rock, Arkansas. As a man, he had no memories of Little Rock—his first memories were of an army wagon train traveling from one fort to another. In 1882 his family was posted to Fort Wingate, New Mexico. Douglas grew up on the American frontier surrounded by bugles, infantrymen, horses, weapons, and Indians. When he died eighty-four years later, rockets were being launched into outer space.

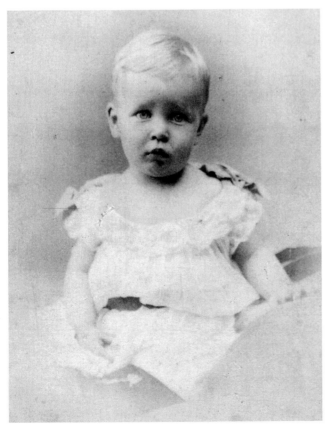

Douglas's brother Malcolm died of measles at age four while on a family trip to Norfolk, Virginia, in April 1883. It had a great effect on his mother, Mary. The rest of her days were devoted to Arthur III and Douglas. On the frontier, she educated them from her husband's voluminous library. She stressed that the "country came first . . . to never lie, never tattle." She wanted her sons to grow up to be like their father or the heroes of the Revolutionary and Civil Wars.

Captain MacArthur's assignments to Forts Wingate and Selden with Company K, 13th Infantry, placed his family at outposts far removed from civilization in the Old West. Douglas MacArthur described it as a "never-ending thrill" and always considered himself to be a "frontiersman" because of his upbringing there. Four years before he was born, Custer and the 7th Cavalry met their doom at Little Big Horn, and in his youth the great Apache chief Geronimo was on the loose in New Mexico.

The MacArthur family poses for a portrait at Fort Selden, New Mexico, in 1886. It was at Fort Selden that Arthur MacArthur finally gained recognition for his efficiency. His Company K was ordered to "civilization" at Fort Leavenworth, Kansas. For the boys that meant the end of the adventure and attending school for the first time, but for Captain MacArthur it was the beginning of a return to the fame he had known in the Civil War.

After three years at Fort Leavenworth, Arthur MacArthur Jr. was promoted to major and the family moved to Washington, where he was assigned to the Army Adjutant General's office. There they lived with the family patriarch, Arthur MacArthur (above), who was serving as a judge for the Supreme Court of the District of Columbia. There were three Arthur MacArthurs living together under one roof.

In 1892 Judge MacArthur was able to secure his grandson Arthur III an appointment to the U.S. Naval Academy in Annapolis, Maryland. A graduate of the class of 1896, he participated in the naval battles off Cuba during the Spanish American War, was one of America's first submarine captains, and was awarded the Navy Cross for distinguished service in the First World War. He held the rank of captain when he died of appendicitis in 1923.

In 1893 Major MacArthur was assigned to the Department of Texas in San Antonio. Douglas was enrolled in the Episcopalian-based West Texas Military Academy, where boys were provided with a "healthful incentive to excel." It was true for Douglas MacArthur. He was quarterback of the football team (left), shortstop for the baseball team, and graduated as valedictorian of the class. His dream of attending the United States Military Academy at West Point seemed a sure thing, but it would not be so easy.

Douglas failed to earn presidential appointments to West Point from Presidents Grover Cleveland and William McKinley, so his mother brought him to Milwaukee where he could study for the competitive exam. It was given in the political district of an old family friend, Congressman Theobald Otjen. Douglas destroyed his competition and earned the appointment. Wearing a white Stetson hat in the left rear of the photo above, he poses with his fellow plebes upon arrival at West Point, New York, in June 1899.

When Douglas MacArthur was accepted to the U.S. Military Academy, his father, Maj. Gen. Arthur MacArthur, was commanding forces in the Philippines fighting against the independence-minded Filipinos. On top of that, his mother came to live in a small hotel next to the academy. Other cadets immediately pegged him as a "momma's boy." He was hazed mercilessly by the upperclassmen, but proved he could take it and was there to stay.

At West Point MacArthur earned the coveted "A" for playing varsity baseball and managed the football team. His senior year he was first captain of the Corps of Cadets and graduated with one of the highest grade point averages ever. On occasion he exhibited a high sensitivity to his sense of honor, but he was well liked by most of his classmates. In the picture below, MacArthur (second from right) is shown with his classmates at graduation in 1903.

An engineering school, West Point's top graduates were assigned to the Engineer Corps. As a young engineer, MacArthur served in the Philippines, was an aide to President Theodore Roosevelt, visited the Panama Canal during its construction, attended the Engineer School in Washington, and worked on projects in the Great Lakes. He also suffered the worst efficiency reports of his career during this time and fought with his superiors over their criticisms of his service.

In 1908 MacArthur was given command of his own company of engineers at Fort Leavenworth. In command of troops was where he showed his forte. With an ability to inspire, the young captain turned Company K from the worst to the best unit of the 3rd Engineer Battalion at Leavenworth. Captain MacArthur is in the front row, second from right, in this photo of the 3rd Battalion staff.

At Fort Leavenworth MacArthur was a much-sought-after demolitions instructor. In the photo above he stands on a bridge as it is blown up for a demonstration.

It was the death of Lt. Gen. Arthur MacArthur (right) that changed the course of Douglas MacArthur's career. When he died in 1912, Arthur was known and revered by many in the U.S. Army. One of his contemporaries was Army Chief of Staff Gen. Leonard Wood. Wood brought Capt. Douglas MacArthur and his mother to Washington, where the young officer could serve as his aide. In Washington's halls of power, Douglas MacArthur was considered an extremely bright and capable officer.

The United States and Mexico came to the brink of war in April 1914. After a U.S. naval contingent was arrested in Tampico, President Woodrow Wilson ordered naval and Marine forces to seize Veracruz. An army brigade was sent under the command of Brig. Gen. Frederick Funston. General Wood was to lead the army if the nation went to war. He needed intelligence about Veracruz and sent thirty-four-year-old Capt. Douglas MacArthur to join Funston's staff. In the photo of the staff above, Funston is seated third from left and MacArthur at the extreme left.

On May 7, 1914, MacArthur ventured 40 miles outside Veracruz in search of locomotives capable of hauling the U.S. Army to Mexico City in the event of war. MacArthur found the locomotives and reported that he killed seven Mexican bandits during his return. The Veracruz provost marshal nominated MacArthur for the Medal of Honor. When the nomination was declined, MacArthur wrote Army Chief of Staff Gen. Hugh Scott, saying the review board had shown "narrow-mindedness" in the rejection.

MacArthur was serving as the Army Press
Censor for the General Staff when President
Wilson called for a declaration of war against the
Central Powers in April 1917. The nation needed
an army of 1 million men, and the Wilson
administration had to institute selective service.
It was MacArthur's job to advocate the necessity
of the draft. He won the loyalty of the press, and
they sold it to the country. His ability was noted
by the Secretary of War, Newton Baker.

A report circulated through the War Department
declaring the General Staff would use only the
Regular Army in the First World War. MacArthur
did not agree. This brought the notice of
Secretary of War Baker. MacArthur explained that
the National Guard had been serving on the
Mexican border the past two years, and the
country needed them. Baker took MacArthur to
see Woodrow Wilson (right), who was convinced
by the major to use the National Guard in the war
in Europe.

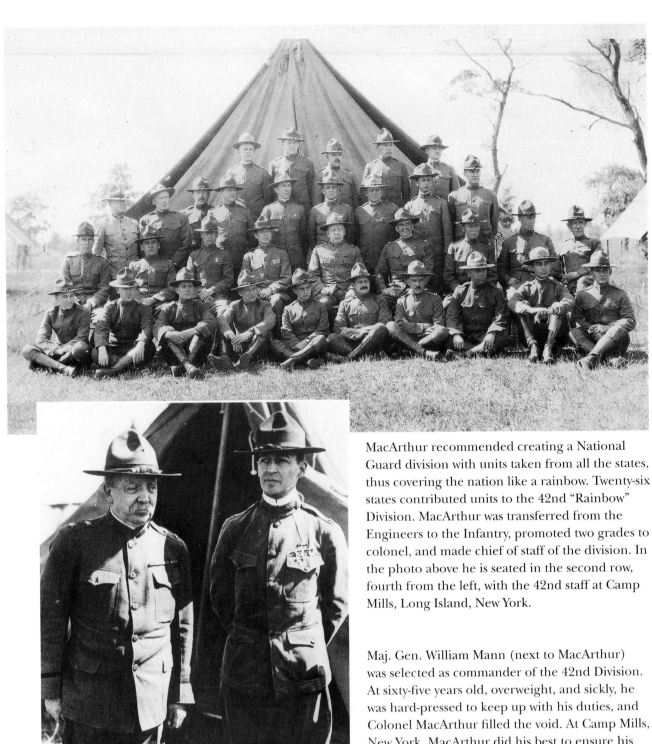

MacArthur recommended creating a National Guard division with units taken from all the states, thus covering the nation like a rainbow. Twenty-six states contributed units to the 42nd "Rainbow" Division. MacArthur was transferred from the Engineers to the Infantry, promoted two grades to colonel, and made chief of staff of the division. In the photo above he is seated in the second row, fourth from the left, with the 42nd staff at Camp Mills, Long Island, New York.

Maj. Gen. William Mann (next to MacArthur) was selected as commander of the 42nd Division. At sixty-five years old, overweight, and sickly, he was hard-pressed to keep up with his duties, and Colonel MacArthur filled the void. At Camp Mills, New York, MacArthur did his best to ensure his division was equipped before embarking for France.

Upon arrival in France, the 42nd was eyed for dissolution and use as replacements by American Expeditionary Force (AEF) commander Gen. John J. Pershing (above). MacArthur cabled Secretary of War Baker, who in turn ordered Pershing to desist from the action. MacArthur saved the division but enraged AEF General Headquarters. Pershing had mixed feelings about the Rainbow Division's chief of staff, saying he "had a high belief in his own abilities," but that he was also his best battlefield commander.

As chief of staff MacArthur did not belong in the front lines, but how could he know the battlefield and his men if he wasn't at the front? He adopted his own personal style, showing up for trench raids carrying no weapons. Promoted to brigadier general in July 1918, he was given the 84th Brigade of the Rainbow Division, leading them in the battles of San Mihiel and the Meuse-Argonne. He was awarded two Distinguished Service Crosses, the Distinguished Service Medal, seven Silver Stars, two Croix de Guerre, and two wound stripes, and earned the epithet of "bravest of the brave" from his men.

Following the war MacArthur was selected to be super-intendent of the U.S. Military Academy and modernize the "monastery on the Hudson." He did his best to end hazing, introduced intramural sports, rid the campus of old, stale professors, and set the academy on a course to train modern officers for the twentieth century.

MacArthur married wealthy socialite Louise Cromwell Brooks in 1922. He proposed to her on the second date and raised the ire of General Pershing. Louise had been involved with Pershing's aide when she met MacArthur. Pershing said he held no grudge, but MacArthur's tenure as superintendent was ended two years early and many of his reforms were undone. Over time they were reinstated, thus making him the father of the modern West Point. The marriage, however, was doomed to failure and ended in divorce in 1928.

Due to his intense love of sports and introduction of the intramural program at West Point, MacArthur was selected as president of the U.S. Olympic team for the 1928 games in the Netherlands. His power to win friends and instill confidence made him a favorite of all the team members.

Following his divorce from Louise, MacArthur returned to the Philippines for his third tour. As commander of the Philippine Department he renewed old acquaintances with prominent Filipinos in the commonwealth. Here he stands with three future presidents: Manuel Quezon, Sergio Osmeña, and Manuel Roxas.

At age fifty, MacArthur was the youngest man to be selected as Chief of Staff of the U.S. Army. Serving energetically during the Great Depression, he preserved the nation's most vital resource: the officer corps. He battled with President Franklin Delano Roosevelt over the budget and saved the corps from being slashed. One of his greatest legacies to the country is that the officer corps trained and led the army that won the Second World War.

Veterans of the First World War marched on Washington in 1932, demanding the bonus that was due to them in 1945. In July, police were ordered to remove the marchers from buildings in downtown Washington. A riot ensued and two men were killed. MacArthur was instructed to send in the army to expel them from downtown. His aide, Maj. Dwight D. Eisenhower, advised him not to accompany the troops. MacArthur feared the army would be blamed if he didn't attend. He showed up in full regalia on July 28, 1932.

MacArthur decided to lead the troops and accept the blame. It was a noble gesture, yet he ignored orders to halt the troops at the Anacostia Bridge leading to the camp of the marchers in Anacostia, Maryland. The camp was destroyed (left) and the Bonus March was over. That night, MacArthur told the press he had just stopped a revolution and called all the First World War veterans communists. It was a horrible choice of words and ruined his reputation with the public.

President Roosevelt signs the Tydings-McDuffie Act in 1934, promising the Philippines their independence in 1945. Manuel Quezon (third from right) was elected as the first president of the commonwealth. Worried about Japanese militarism and expansion in China, Quezon asked General MacArthur to come to the Philippines at the end of his term as chief of staff and to build a defense force for the archipelago.

MacArthur and his aides, T. J. Davis (extreme left) and Dwight D. Eisenhower (third from left), are welcomed on the docks of Manila in October 1935. The previous month MacArthur, his eighty-three-year-old mother, and a small staff embarked for the Philippines on the USS *Hoover*. On the journey across the Pacific he met thirty-seven-year-old Tennessee native Jean Marie Faircloth (right). Only weeks after arriving, his mother died in Manila. His lifelong confidant gone, MacArthur turned to Jean.

MacArthur's contract as military advisor to the Philippine Commonwealth stated he be given the rank of Field Marshal of the Philippine Army. Davis, MacArthur, and Eisenhower are seen prior to the ceremony (left), and MacArthur stands with the Quezons on August 26, 1936 (above). Eisenhower thought it was a farce. Over time he became disenchanted with the defense project, prospects for his future, and General MacArthur. Eisenhower left MacArthur's staff in 1939.

Little support for the Philippine defense project was forthcoming from either the United States or the Philippines. Many in the War Department believed MacArthur's effort was a waste of time and money. He was ordered back to the United States in 1937 to take a two-star command. Instead, he retired from the army.

Living at the Manila Hotel with his wife, Jean, and only son, Arthur IV, MacArthur built a "paper army" and grew discouraged, yearning for something more. The Japanese made sure he would have what he wished for.

In the winter and spring of 1941, Philippine Department commander Maj. Gen. George E. Grunert (above right) began advocating the federalization of the Philippine Army for the war he believed was coming. If the Philippine Army was to indeed be federalized, MacArthur wanted command. Quezon was making it known the military mission was to be terminated, and MacArthur was telling friends in Washington that if he didn't get the job he would return to the United States.

The War Department had little faith in a successful defense of the Philippines, but Chief of Staff of the U.S. Army Gen. George C. Marshall (seated center) was changing his mind. His air planners, foremost among them Maj. Gen. Henry "Hap" Arnold (fourth from left), were pitching a new wonder weapon: the Boeing B-17. A long-range bomber, it was a weapon Marshall thought could deter Japanese ambitions in Southeast Asia, and he envisioned a new command in the Philippines. In June 1941, Marshall told MacArthur to sit tight.

Japan seized all of French Indochina in 1941, taking control of airfields and naval facilities. President Roosevelt froze Japanese assets and imposed an oil embargo on Japan. Oil was the lifeblood of the Japanese Empire, and its predominant source was the United States. Secretary of War Henry Stimson and General Marshall (left) immediately saw how vulnerable the Philippines now were. The archipelago straddled Japan's sea lanes to the oil-rich Dutch East Indies.

Almost overnight, strengthening the Philippines became a priority. President Roosevelt, Secretary Stimson, and General Marshall were all wary of MacArthur, but to each of them there was no other choice for commander in the Philippines. He had more knowledge of Asia than any other officer in the U.S. Army. On July 26, 1941, MacArthur was recalled to active duty as commander of the United States Army Forces in the Far East (USAFFE). He reads his orders to the press in the picture above.

At Zablan Field MacArthur inducts the Philippine forces into the service of the United States. All of them took the oath of loyalty, stating: "I do solemnly swear that I will bear true faith and allegiance to the United States of America, that I will serve them honestly and faithfully against all their enemies whomsoever; and that I will obey the order of the President of the United States and the orders of the officers appointed over me according to the rules and articles of war."

Prior to MacArthur's recall, Quezon wouldn't even see the general, convinced his military defense program for the Philippines was a waste of effort and money. At one point MacArthur said, "There will come a time when the President will want to see me more than I want to see him." Now was the time. Quezon pledged his undying support and put all the resources of the Philippines at the general's disposal.

Throughout the 1920s and 1930s, the United States had neglected the defenses of the Philippines. Now MacArthur had to ready the nation for war. When assessing the problem, his chief of staff remarked, "It's almost an insurmountable task." MacArthur's reply, which became a propaganda tool for the United States during the war, was, "I can but do my best." His first move was to choose the staff to help him.

Col. Richard K. Sutherland was MacArthur's chief of staff. Like his predecessor, Dwight D. Eisenhower, he had the ability to transform MacArthur's ideas into concise orders.

Col. Richard J. Marshall was deputy chief of staff. With a bright mind for logistics, he was handpicked by MacArthur for duty in the Philippines.

Col. Hugh Casey was chief engineer. War in the Pacific was going to be an engineer's war, and he was one of MacArthur's most brilliant officers.

Brig. Gen. Spencer Akin arrived in the islands just before war broke out. As MacArthur's signal officer, he was also the chief code breaker.

Col. Charles A. Willoughby was intelligence officer, a position he would retain through the Korean War.

As USAFFE commander MacArthur controlled Grunert's Philippine Department and its military arm, the Philippine Division, Regular Army troops commanded by Maj. Gen. Jonathan Wainwright. The 31st Infantry Regiment (seen above, marching out of the old Spanish walled city of Intramuros) was the only all-American infantry unit in the Philippines. It was from the ranks of the 31st that MacArthur took officers to train the Philippine Army.

The bulk of the Philippine Division was made up of Philippine Scouts. The 26th Cavalry and 45th and 57th Infantry Regiments were Filipino soldiers commanded by American officers. It was a privilege to be a Scout, and after six months of training it was difficult to tell the difference between a recruit and a veteran. MacArthur's plan for training the Philippine Army was based on this concept, and it was the reason for his conviction that he would be ready for war by April 1942. When the Philippine Army was mobilized in September 1941, the six-month period ended in March 1942.

Maj. Gen. George Moore's U.S. Army Harbor and Defense Command also came under MacArthur's control. The U.S. 59th and 60th and the 91st and 92nd Philippine Scout Coast Artillery units manned the defenses of Corregidor and Forts Drum, Frank, and Hughes. Corregidor's 12-inch (above) and Fort Drum's 14-inch batteries (below) were constructed to destroy any fleet entering Manila Bay. Nearly 5,000 men were assigned to the command. Their aerial defense capabilities, however, were extremely lacking.

New recruits of the Philippine Army's 61st Division stand in parade formation on the island of Negros. The bulk of USAFFE were Filipinos. MacArthur told the War Department he had 20,000 Filipinos trained and ready at the time of their federalization. It wasn't so; the Philippine Army was a force on paper. MacArthur planned to create 10 divisions of 10,000 men each by April 1942. They were deficient in everything: training, equipment, weapons, supplies, and artillery.

Biplanes of the Philippine Army Air Corps (PAAC) are pictured in front of a hangar at Camp Murphy, the PAAC flying school. The PAAC was completely inadequate, flying obsolete planes that were no match for anything the Japanese had. Philippine pilots were brave, eager, and ready to prove themselves, even though they were few in number.

A Philippine "Q-boat" races across Manila Bay in March 1939. The U.S. Navy's Asiatic Fleet submarine, S-41, is in the background. The Philippine navy was almost nonexistent. During his years as military advisor, MacArthur championed a fleet of torpedo boats to defend the islands. Only three were available by 1941.

A new element to Hart's command was the arrival of Motor Torpedo Boat Squadron (MTB) 3 in September 1941. Arriving on the freighter USS *Guadalupe*, the squadron was made up of six boats. MacArthur asked MTB-3, based at Cavite Naval Base in Manila Bay, to train Filipino crews for the Philippine navy's three torpedo boats.

Manila was home port to the U.S. Navy's Asiatic Fleet, whose largest capital ship was the cruiser USS *Houston*. Adm. Thomas Hart (left) was the fleet commander. He had been a close friend of MacArthur's brother, but his relationship with the general was strained. Hart saw him as reclusive and at one point labeled MacArthur's overly optimistic attitude as "not all together sane." At a time when the Army and Navy command should have been working arduously together, MacArthur and Hart could not get along.

One of the first P-40 fighter planes to arrive in the Philippines sits on the runway at Clark Field in 1941. The American Army Air Corps was the key element for the push to reinforce the Philippines. The War Department planned to place 272 bombers in the islands with two pursuit groups of P-40 fighter planes. It was believed air power could halt Japanese expansion into Southeast Asia and defend the island against invasion.

Philippine Department commander Major General Grunert (at right) stands with the air corps commander in the Philippines, Brig. Gen. Henry Clagett, in the fall of 1941. The War Department felt Clagett was sickly and generally unfit for the larger command being created. MacArthur was presented with a choice of replacements. Maj. Gen. Lewis Brereton was selected to command the newly created Far East Air Force (FEAF).

When Brereton (left) heard the plan to send bombers to the Philippines, he recognized it as a foolish proposition. Radar, antiaircraft artillery, and even landing fields were scarce. Where were all these planes destined for the islands to be stationed? Brereton let his superiors in the War Department know his skepticism, and he was told that all would be forthcoming.

There was only one airfield in the Philippines that could handle the weight of a B-17: Clark Field north of Manila. Engineer units feverishly worked to expand Clark's runways to accommodate all the bombers due to arrive in the islands. The 19th and 27th Bomb Groups were scheduled to arrive before the new year.

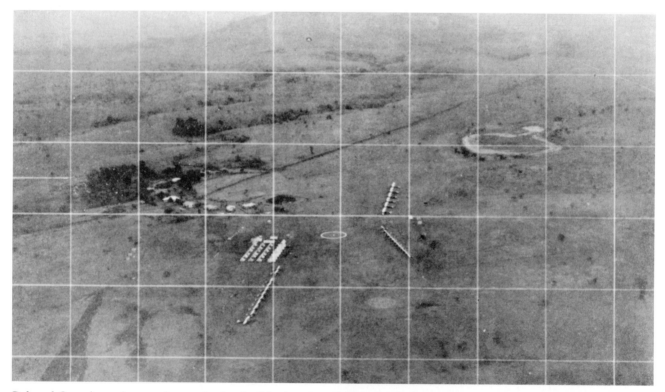

Colonel Casey's engineers also worked to build a bomber field at the Del Monte pineapple plantation on the southernmost island of Mindanao (above). High on the Bukidnon Plain, its soil could handle the weight of the B-17. It didn't matter. Of all the planes destined for the Philippines, only thirty-five B-17s and seventy-five P-40s were present in the islands before the war began.

MacArthur and his chief of staff Brig. Gen. Richard Sutherland bid farewell to Major General Grunert. The formation of USAFFE meant there was no longer a need for the Philippine Department. MacArthur was loath to absorb the department with Grunert still around, so in October he had the general sent stateside. He was getting rid of a capable officer who knew the men and the islands.

General MacArthur stands with Maj. Gen. Jonathan Wainwright, wearing a campaign hat, at the Philippine Division maneuvers in October 1941. Grunert's departure meant that Wainwright was now the senior field commander. He was a hard-driving, hard-drinking cavalryman and like MacArthur believed in an active, mobile defense rather than the siege mentality dictated by the American plan for war in the Philippines, known as War Plan Orange.

Prewar plans by the U.S. military were accorded colors, and war against Japan was labeled War Plan Orange. As it pertained to the Philippines, the plan was to concentrate U.S. and Philippine forces on the main island of Luzon and retreat to the peninsula of Bataan, the island fortress of Corregidor, and the harbor forts. There they could deny Japan the use of Manila Bay and the port facilities in Manila and hold out until relieved by the U.S. Navy.

MacArthur viewed War Plan Orange as defeatist and called for a defense of the entire archipelago by halting any Japanese invasion at the beaches. When FEAF commander Brereton arrived in the Philippines, he brought word that the War Department approved MacArthur's ideas of a mobile defense to defend all the islands, not just Luzon.

Maj. Gen. William F. Sharp (at left above) was given the Visayan-Mindanao command, with control of a multitude of islands to the south of Luzon. On Luzon, the main island, MacArthur split his troops into the North and South Luzon Forces.

MacArthur visits maneuvers conducted by the Philippine Division in October 1941. He never displayed anything but confidence. Vociferous about his faith in the Philippine Army, he was also convincing in the idea that he could defend the islands. He wasn't blind though; MacArthur knew the deficiencies in his forces. He wrote his commanders that training was lacking and time could not be wasted. Time was one thing there wasn't enough of.

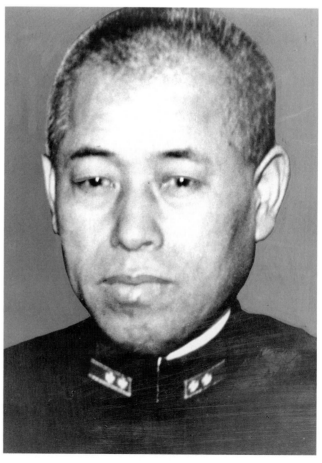

Gen. Tojo Hideki (1884–1948) was selected as prime minister of Japan in October 1941. Japan was being strangled by the U.S. oil embargo. Its diplomatic mission in Washington, under Adm. Kichisaburo Nomura, was negotiating with U.S. Secretary of State Cordell Hull over the issue, but the United States demanded Japan withdraw from China and Indochina. A supporter of the Tripartite Pact with Nazi Germany and a former commander in China, Hideki believed that Japan should go to war rather than withdraw. In November 1941, his desires were approved by Emperor Hirohito.

Adm. Isoroku Yamamoto's plan to strike the United States at its naval base at Pearl Harbor was Japan's opening move to control the Pacific. Yamamoto lived in the United States in the 1920s and had seen its size and industry. More than any other Japanese, he knew what the cost of war with the United States would be. He felt there were few scenarios where the outcome was victory, but there was no other choice, and the best chance was predicated on a surprise attack. While Nomura talked in Washington, Japanese forces trained religiously.

The Nomura–Hull talks broke down at the end of November, and the War Department sent a war warning to all its commanders. MacArthur responded that he was ready, whether he believed it or not. The dice were being rolled, and it would all be played out. Japanese planes were making feints over the islands. On December 5, MacArthur gave a shoot-down order against any plane over Philippine air space.

# CHAPTER 3
# THE PHILIPPINES CAMPAIGN
## DECEMBER 1941–MARCH 1942

Pilots of the Japanese 3rd Kokutai are seen on Formosa prior to their attacks on the Philippines. Due to the international dateline, it was December 8 in the Philippines when the Japanese attacked Pearl Harbor. Japanese naval and army air forces on the island of Formosa were supposed to attack the Philippines shortly after the attack on Pearl Harbor but were grounded by fog.

The USS *Wasp* explodes and the USS *Arizona* sinks during the Japanese attack on Pearl Harbor. The Japanese diplomatic mission in Washington asked for an audience with Secretary of State Cordell Hull on the morning of December 7. The plan was to present Washington with a declaration of war just as its navy struck the American base at Pearl Harbor. They failed. The attack came with no warning or declaration of war. As Yamamoto feared, Pearl Harbor awoke a sleeping giant.

Controversy surrounds the morning of December 8 in the Philippines, and Brig. Gen. Richard K. Sutherland (left) is at the heart of it. Sutherland got word of the attack on Pearl at 3:30 AM and immediately informed MacArthur. Both then met at headquarters. At 5:00 AM, General Brereton asked for permission to launch a bombing raid on Formosa. Sutherland denied Brereton access to MacArthur. The reason why has never been explained.

The Japanese bombed the southern city of Davao and the northern cities of Baguio and Aparri early on the 8th. Then the American radar station at Iba Field on north Luzon (right) picked up incoming flights. All the planes of the 19th Bomb Group and 20th Pursuit Squadron at Clark Field went into the air, but nothing happened. At 10:00 AM, Brereton was again turned away at headquarters, but at 10:15 MacArthur ordered him to conduct reconnaissance flights over Formosa. At 11:30 AM, all the B-17s and P-40s of the 20th and 17th Pursuit Squadrons were ordered back to Clark Field.

Iba Airfield, home to the 3rd Pursuit Squadron and the only working radar in the Philippines.

The fog cleared over eastern Formosa after dawn on December 8, and the Japanese army air forces hit Baguio and Aparri. At 10:00 AM the fog cleared over western Formosa, and the Japanese naval bombers and fighters were able to take off and arrive over Clark Field just after all the American airplanes had returned to base and were lined up to refuel.

Clark Field was hit at 12:30 PM by high-level bombers and then low-level strafing by Zero fighters. It was completely destroyed in a matter of thirty minutes. Unbelievably, Clark Field was without proper air cover at its most vulnerable time. Like at Pearl Harbor, luck was with the Japanese. Half of the B-17 bomber force was caught on the ground at Clark Field. Most were destroyed. All were put out of action in the Japanese attack.

The FEAF was reeling and its ability to resist the Japanese air assault was limited. On December 10, the Japanese bombed Nichol's Field, home of the 17th Pursuit Squadron, south of Manila. For the third time they were thorough in their job.

Cavite Naval Station, home to the 16th Naval District and the base for the U.S. Navy's Asiatic Fleet, burns after a Japanese air assault. Hart's fleet moved to the southern Philippines before the war, but all the facilities, submarines, torpedo boats, and an array of miscellaneous ships were still at Cavite when the Japanese struck on December 10. The base was reduced to ruins after the Japanese finished their raids.

There was little to be proud of, but morale was the key to a prolonged defense in the Philippines. At his headquarters at Fort Santiago in Manila's ancient walled city of Intramuros, MacArthur made Philippine pilot Jesús Villamor a national hero, decorating him with the Distinguished Service Cross for bravery.

MacArthur gave command of the North Luzon Force to Wainwright (left) and the South Luzon Force to Maj. Gen. George Parker. In the days following the destruction at Clark Field and Cavite Naval Station, the Japanese made landings at various points on Luzon and Mindanao. Then 2,500 Japanese of the 16th Division landed southeast of Manila at Legaspi on December 12. Parker's South Luzon Force moved to face them. Wainwright's North Luzon Force watched and waited.

The Japanese brought nearly eighty transports into Lingayen Gulf, a few hundred miles north of Manila. There was no Far East Air Force left to oppose them, and Brereton was on his way to Australia. Admiral Hart's fleet was on its way to Java, but of his twenty-nine submarines only six made it to Lingayen, and they were armed with defective torpedoes. The landings began on December 21.

Untrained Philippine Army troops of the North Luzon Force moved north to defend their homeland. The force was described as little more than a mob. The 26th Cavalry were mounted on horses and used scout cars like the one seen at left. The 26th Cavalry and two tank battalions of the Provisional Tank Group, equipped with eighty light tanks and thirty-four half-tracks, backed up the Filipinos.

Lt. Gen. Masaharu Homma, commander of the Japanese Fourteenth Area Army, came ashore at Lingayen on December 24. Homma spoke English fluently and was a poet. He also boasted that Japan was "willing to sacrifice ten million to win the war; how many were the Americans prepared to lose?"

Japanese troops quickly dispatched USAFFE defenses at the beach. The Philippine 71st Division, under Brig. Gen. Clyde Selleck, almost ceased to exist. Japanese were now advancing against the Americans and Filipinos from the north as well as south of Manila.

MacArthur immediately reverted to War Plan Orange and ordered retreat into the Bataan Peninsula and the island fortress of Corregidor. Seen above, Corregidor was a tadpole-shaped island and Bataan was a peninsula dominated by mountains. Over 14,000 personnel tried to find space on Corregidor and nearly 100,000 on Bataan.

General MacArthur and his wife, Jean, are pictured on Corregidor shortly after their arrival on the island on Christmas Eve 1941. Jean had decided not to leave the Philippines when most of the military wives left in the summer of 1941. She resolved that she would share the fate of her husband, saying, "We three drink of the same cup."

After arriving on the island, the MacArthurs lived on the high western plateau known as Topside. The house was destroyed in the first bombing raid, and MacArthur barely escaped death himself. After the first raid, the family moved to a house about a mile from the eastern portal of the Malinta Tunnel, within quick driving distance when necessary.

Men play cards outside and then run for Malinta Tunnel at the sound of the air raid signal. The Japanese made their first of many aerial bombing raids on Corregidor on December 29. Carved out of Malinta Hill on Corregidor's Bottomside Area, Malinta Tunnel was over 800 feet long and 24 feet wide. With laterals slanting off the main tunnels, it had office space, kitchens, and a hospital that could house thousands.

A Japanese Type 89 tank moves south down Highway 3 from Lingayen Gulf toward Manila. While Homma was pushing Wainwright's forces south, the Japanese 16th Division was on the heels of Parker's forces pushing north. Though destroyed at each encounter, the withdrawing USAFFE forces made the Japanese hesitate in the chase. Homma's greatest mistake, however, was thinking Manila was the prize. He focused on taking the city and gave USAFFE forces the time to complete the withdrawal into Bataan.

A strategic withdrawal in the face of the enemy is one of the hardest maneuvers in warfare, but the reversion to War Plan Orange required it for the retreat into Bataan. The plan was for Wainwright to retire to a series of prepared defenses and hold off the Japanese pressing from the north while the South Luzon Force poured into Bataan. Wainwright would follow them.

Before leaving for Corregidor, MacArthur declared Manila an open city so it would not face destruction in a deadly fight for the city. Homma's army moved into the city unopposed and established control.

The University of Santo Tomas was one of the oldest Catholic universities in Asia. It was chosen as the site for the concentration of all Allied civilians in Manila. When the Japanese arrived in the city on January 2, the roundup of civilians began. They were told to pack enough for three days, not realizing they would spend the next three years confined to the Santo Tomas Internment Camp.

Lieutenant General Homma stands with Quezon's confidante, Jorge Vargas. Initially, it was Vargas who took control of the Philippine government under the occupation. He said Quezon and MacArthur told him to cooperate—he was told to go along but to never sign an oath of loyalty or actively aid the Japanese.

After the South Luzon Force made it into Bataan, Wainwright's North Force crossed into the peninsula. At Layac junction, the main entrance into Bataan, USAFFE forces tried to hold off their Japanese pursuers and took a serious beating. Artilleryman Jose Calugas of the Philippine 78th Artillery (left) earned the Medal of Honor for action at Layac. With most of the Philippine army's artillery knocked out, Calugas single-handedly operated a 75mm piece against all odds.

The jungle hides the defenders of Bataan (below). War Plan Orange envisioned 40,000 effectives in Bataan with food stocks to support that many for 6 months. Medicine should have been stockpiled and civilians evacuated, but that wasn't the reality. Over 100,000 people were on Bataan, and all needed to be fed. Dengue fever and malaria were rife and medicine a luxury. The command went on half rations almost immediately.

Men of the 31st Infantry avoid artillery fire in a slit trench on Bataan. USAFFE forces held the Abucay Line, running east to west across Bataan. MacArthur divided the command on Bataan into the I Corps under Major General Wainwright to the west and the II Corps under General Parker to the east.

Exhaustion takes hold of a motorcycle dispatch rider on Bataan.

On January 10, MacArthur visited Bataan. He spent ten hours on the peninsula and both met with corps commanders and visited with the troops. He told them all what Washington was telling him: "Help is on the way." His presence on the peninsula was a rarity. Everyone knew about his reputation in the First World War as a front-line general, but before long the men on Bataan would call him "Dugout Doug." It stung the sixty-two-year-old MacArthur, who had proven himself on numerous battlefields in his life.

MacArthur exits Malinta Tunnel with Brigadier General Sutherland. Everyone on Corregidor saw the general—called "Dugout Doug" on Bataan—go for his daily walk when the shelling was heaviest. He visited gun emplacements when they were under fire. No one on Corregidor called him "Dugout Doug." In Malinta Tunnel, MacArthur maintained contact with Washington and the War Department. He bombarded his superiors with message after message on the dire situation in the Philippines, repeatedly asking for support, supplies, anything.

MacArthur issued his "Help is on the Way" message on January 15, 1942, and ordered it read to all the troops on Bataan. It is one of the most controversial episodes of the campaign. Many believe he was lying to the men to build morale just before the Japanese offensive on the Abucay Line. Had he signed the message with the names of George Marshall and Franklin Roosevelt, it would not have been a lie—everything he told his men was what Washington was telling him. The question is, did he believe it?

On January 19 it was found the Japanese 9th Infantry had made its way across Mt. Natib in the center of the Abucay Line and established a roadblock behind the II Corps' 51st Division. This led to the evacuation of I and II Corps farther south to a new line of defense. There was now nowhere else to retreat. Tank traps of the defenses are seen above. Weary but undefeated men of a Signal Corps unit line up for mess call in the photo below.

In January and February 1942, elements of the Japanese 20th Regiment of the 16th Division attempted to overwhelm the USAFFE forces by landing at their rear on the west coast of Bataan, initiating the Battle of the Points. At the same time, infiltration in the II Corps' front created pockets of Japanese behind the main line of resistance. Their elimination became the Battle of the Pockets.

Here, Longoskwayan Point juts into the ocean on the western coast of Bataan, where the 20th Regiment disembarked in late January 1942. The Japanese held onto the area tenaciously.

Air Corps personnel were issued rifles and made infantrymen to face the Japanese in the Battle of the Points. Everyone available—air corps and naval personnel—had to be thrown into the fight to hold the Japanese to the coastal areas.

The untrained provisional infantry handled themselves well until the professionals showed up. Japanese defenders on the Points fought to the death when the 45th and 57th Philippine Scouts and elements of the 4th Marines moved in to clean up the mess in late February. Here, Philippine scouts pose with a captured sword.

The Battle of the Pockets was another fight to the death and wore out both the Americans and the Japanese. In a vicious two-week struggle, the Philippine 11th Division played a pivotal role in destroying the Japanese infiltrators and earned a Presidential Unit Citation. As the photo shows, fighting was brutal and revolting.

Airmen of the 24th Pursuit Group pose with the last P-40E at Bataan Field. Like the soldiers and sailors, despite the odds the air corps continued to take on the Japanese. In early March the last few P-40s launched a raid on Subic Bay, inflicting losses on Japanese naval forces.

Inadequate for the numbers they served and working with a bare minimum of supplies, the kitchens on Bataan were struggling to feed the men. Everything that moved was eaten on Bataan: snakes, monkeys, water buffalo, and rats. By the end of February, they had eaten all the horses of the 26th Cavalry. The calorie intake was never enough, and malnutrition was commonplace.

American troops prepare to throw Molotov cocktails in the defense of Bataan. Despite conditions, in January and February 1942 USAFFE fought the Japanese to a standstill at the battles of the Points and the Pockets. A lull came over the battlefield. The British defense at Singapore, however, collapsed on February 15, 1942. It wouldn't be long before the Japanese brought in reinforcements to the Philippines.

Mass is held in a lateral of the Malinta Tunnel in March 1942. On Corregidor, the only places to go during bombardment were the Malinta Tunnel and gun emplacements. Many a man lost his composure over fear of leaving the tunnel. Corregidor was better stocked with supplies—prompting begrudging remarks by many of the men on Bataan about the "tunnel rats" living on the island fortress—but all were suffering.

Manuel Quezon and his wife and daughter pose on Corregidor with Jean and Arthur. Whether it was causing MacArthur's delay to act at the beginning of the war, inspiring his order against seizing rice stocks during the retreat into Bataan, or voicing his reluctance to obliterate the inhabited Cavite area when Japanese artillery was beginning to use it, Quezon influenced and affected MacArthur's generalship. To ensure a government in exile, the president and his family left Corregidor by submarine on February 20. He gave this picture to the MacArthurs before departing, signing it, "May we all meet again and soon, Manuel Quezon." Washington had decided. The end was coming.

On February 22, 1942, President Roosevelt ordered MacArthur to proceed to Mindanao, the southernmost island of the Philippine archipelago, and from there to Australia, where he was to head a new command. Australian prime minister John Curtin, having no faith in Great Britain to help the cause of Australia, looked to MacArthur to cement the defense of the continent with American support.

MacArthur and his chief of staff Sutherland sit at their desks in Lateral Three of Malinta Tunnel, the location of USAFFE headquarters during the siege of Bataan and Corregidor. Washington's order to leave Corregidor meant MacArthur had to leave his troops to surrender and worse. Washington gave him the authority to choose the time and manner of his departure.

Jean and Arthur were ordered out along with Sutherland. MacArthur was going to a new command in Australia, the purpose of which he believed was to relieve the Philippines. He wanted to arrive with a staff he could immediately set to the task, so he had Sutherland make a list of staff members to accompany him.

From left to right: Colonel Willoughby, Brig. Gen. Spencer Akin, an unknown officer, Maj. Joe Sherr, and Maj. P. R. Wing stand in front of the Signal Corps headquarters on Bataan. Willoughby, MacArthur's intelligence officer, was on Sutherland's list of staff to accompany the general, and so were Akin and Sherr, a genius and Akin's number-one code breaker. Their subordinates, just like the Navy's code-breaking unit on Corregidor, were removed by submarine to Australia.

Maj. Gen. Edward P. King (far left) stands on Corregidor with an unknown officer on March 10, 1942. Two men that would not accompany MacArthur were Wainwright and King. Wainwright took over on Corregidor as commander of the forces on Luzon, and King was made the commander of the troops on Bataan. King had been the chief of artillery on Bataan, praised most highly in the campaign by MacArthur. Named commander of a forlorn hope, he had little reason for optimism.

Brigadier General Sutherland, Col. Lewis E. Beebe, and an unknown officer sit in a lounge area set up outside Malinta Tunnel. Beebe was chosen to be MacArthur's chief of staff remaining on Corregidor. MacArthur didn't want any one commander having control of all the USAFFE forces. He would command from Australia through Beebe. The surrender of one command, therefore, couldn't force the surrender of the others. It was a setup that was immediately ignored by Washington; Wainwright was the commander of the Philippines.

Lt. John Bulkeley was the commander of MTB-3. MacArthur asked Bulkeley to break through the Japanese blockade and take him to the island of Mindanao. Having lost all his personal effects when Cavite was destroyed, by March 1942 Bulkeley had long hair bound by a bandana, a beard and mustache, an oilcloth slicker, and two pistols and a knife tucked into his belt. He was what legends are made of, and MacArthur trusted him to take him through the blockade.

The PT-32 and its sister torpedo boats were 80-foot vessels powered by three Packard engines that gorged themselves on gasoline. The Packards supplied the boats with their power, and torpedoes and machine guns provided their punch. Tainted fuel gave the fuel lines hell; the engines could be overhauled and reworked only so much with no new parts, lubricants, or other supplies. PT-32 was the only boat of the four to not survive the journey.

Bulkeley's PT-41 was the boat the MacArthurs took on the 500-mile journey to Mindanao. In the days prior to the secret departure date, MacArthur and his wife went for a test ride around Corregidor. On the evening of March 11, the boat picked up the MacArthur family at the north dock of Corregidor. MacArthur bid Wainwright goodbye at the dock and said he would return.

This souvenir photo honors the officers involved with the escape from Corregidor. While Bulkeley picked up MacArthur, the other three boats picked up the staff from Mariveles Harbor on Bataan. They ran in formation leaving Manila Bay, then lost contact with each other in the rough seas of the archipelago. By circumstance and luck they evaded the blockade, and all but the PT-32 boat and its crew made it to Mindanao. The journey forged a bond between MacArthur and his staff, and for the rest of World War II and beyond he would be served loyally by members of this "Bataan Gang."

MacArthur decorated Lieutenant Bulkeley and his men with the Silver Star for their part in the run to Mindanao. Bulkeley was awarded the Medal of Honor for his efforts in the Philippines throughout the campaign. In a navy full of animosity toward MacArthur, Bulkeley was always a firm supporter of the general.

Rear Adm. James Rockwell and Visayan-Mindanao commander Maj. Gen. William Sharp converse at the Del Monte Plantation after the PT boat journey. Rockwell was commander of the 16th Naval District in Manila; the navy requested his presence on the escape. Sharp met MacArthur on the pier at Cagayan de Oro on Mindanao's north coast when PT-41 arrived on the morning of March 13. MacArthur spent time with Sharp, instructing him to engage in guerrilla warfare should surrender come.

Lt. Col. Charles Morhouse made the trip because he was a doctor. Jean wanted one on the journey in case something happened to Arthur. Morhouse was serving with the air corps troops on Bataan, was picked off a list, and ended up in the PT-41 boat with the MacArthurs.

Maj. Sidney Huff made the journey on the PT-41 boat with MacArthur. Years later Huff recounted how MacArthur kept him up the night of March 11 going over the entire Philippine campaign, beginning with his time as military advisor to the Philippine Commonwealth and reviewing the mistakes and what could have been done. The general was wracked with seasickness the entire journey and tortured by the reality that he had left his command in the face of the enemy.

MacArthur, Sutherland, and Brig. Gen. Richard J. Marshall are seen at the Del Monte airstrip on Mindanao waiting for the B-17s to take them to Australia. The first ones that arrived were decrepit, and MacArthur radioed Australia that he wanted four brand-new ones to come to Del Monte. Two B-17s arrived on March 16, and the entire party loaded up and began the last leg of the journey to Australia: 1,400 air miles from Del Monte to Darwin.

The flight from Del Monte brought the MacArthur party to Batchelor Field in Darwin, Australia, but Japanese bombers were following close behind. Everyone boarded planes and flew to the arid interior of the continent. Here the MacArthurs are met at Alice Springs. MacArthur wears a white hat because his famous khaki hat shrank on the PT boat journey. Jean didn't think Arthur could take any more flying, so they decided to go by train from Alice Springs.

Brig. Gen. Patrick Hurley stands with General
MacArthur in Alice Springs, Australia, on March 18,
1942. In Australia, Hurley's job was to get blockade-
running ships into the Philippines. It was an endeavor
that failed, but not from lack of effort. Hurley offered
the general his plane to fly his family to Melbourne, but
they chose the train to Adelaide on the south coast.
MacArthur knew Hurley well and had worked closely
with him during his chief of staff days. Apparently,
however, their meeting in Alice Springs was tense, as
afterward Hurley remarked that he couldn't
understand why MacArthur was so angry.

One of a series of small, narrow-gauge trains that took
the MacArthurs, Sutherland, Huff, Morhouse, and the
nanny from Alice Springs to Adelaide. It had a
passenger car and a dining car and had to stop to allow
the passengers to go to the dining car. On the long,
bumpy ride south, MacArthur theorized how he would
soon return to the Philippines. Jean said it was the first
time he really slept since leaving Corregidor.

At Terowie, just a few hundred miles from Adelaide,
reporters met MacArthur as the train arrived. He stated
that the president ordered him to Australia to organize
an offensive to relieve the Philippines. "I came through
and I shall return," he said. Gen. Richard Marshall, who
flew ahead to Melbourne and returned, informed
MacArthur there was no force in Australia to relieve the
Philippines. MacArthur's confidence faltered.

MacArthur arrived at Melbourne's Spencer Station on March 21, 1942. A commonwealth of Great Britain, Australia expected support from its parent country, but Singapore had already surrendered and the British were barely holding on against the Nazis in Europe. Though despondent of the situation he now knew existed, MacArthur's arrival signaled U.S. support, and he exuded nothing but confidence to the people. At Spencer Station MacArthur launched a thunderbolt at his superiors saying, "No general can make something out of nothing. My success or failure will depend primarily upon the resources . . . place[d] at my disposal."

Douglas MacArthur stands with Prime Ministers Peter Frazer of New Zealand and John Curtin of Australia. These two men lobbied for MacArthur's removal from the Philippines and his appointment as Supreme Commander of Allied forces to face the Japanese.

General MacArthur and John Curtin huddle together after his arrival in Melbourne. Curtin was a labor leader jailed for opposing involvement in the First World War. MacArthur was a conservative, capitalist warrior. They forged an unlikely partnership to project power outside Australia. As long as victory was achieved, their positions were solid. Curtin said to MacArthur, "You have been chosen to lead a great cause, the results of which mean everything to the future of mankind."

The Allies were reeling in defeat while the USAFFE was still fighting. A hero was needed, and MacArthur became the propaganda piece. He was awarded the Medal of Honor on March 24, 1942, at the urging of President Roosevelt, and became a household name in the world of the Allies.

On April 18, 1942, an order was issued delineating the command structure for the Pacific. Adm. Chester Nimitz was given command of the Pacific Ocean Area, encompassing the Central and South Pacific Theaters, and MacArthur was given the Southwest Pacific Area (SWPA). The Allied strategy was to defeat the Nazis in Europe first while fighting a strategic defensive in the Pacific. MacArthur never supported the "Europe First" mentality or the decision against unifying command in the Pacific.

Distance was the dominating factor in the Southwest Pacific—battles here were measured by the hundreds if not thousands of miles. There were no roads to Tokyo and victory; the highway of the Pacific was water.

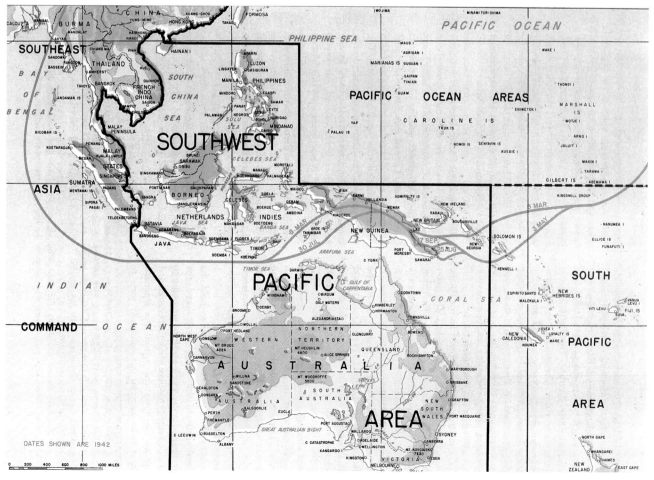

MacArthur is shown with his Allied Land Forces commander, Australian general Sir Thomas Blamey. There were few American combat troops in Australia. The U.S. 32nd and 41st Infantry Divisions were en route, but they would need to be trained. The forces MacArthur had were predominantly Australian, so an Australian was chosen to command in the field. The U.S. War Department and General Marshall urged MacArthur to place Australian officers within his staff and throughout headquarters; it was advice he never followed.

A month after MacArthur's escape from Corregidor, General King surrendered the force on Bataan. After a weeklong Japanese offensive, the starving, disease-ridden Filipinos and Americans were overrun by fresh troops, veterans of the victory over the British at Singapore. MacArthur ordered Wainwright not to surrender on Bataan, but King saw disaster with further resistance and capitulated on April 9. In the photo above, General King, Maj. Wade Cothran, and Maj. Achille Tisdelle discuss the terms of the surrender of Bataan. When King asked the Japanese for consideration of his men, the response was, "We are not barbarians."

American prisoners of war await their future under Japanese guard. Over 75,000 surrendered on Bataan and were forced on a 65-mile march from Bataan to the town of San Fernando, where they boarded overloaded boxcars for a ride north and the final march to the prison camp at Camp O'Donnell. Few were allowed water or food, and atrocities were commonplace. It is estimated that 5,000 died from Japanese brutality and neglect on what is now known as the Bataan Death March.

The Japanese staged this photo at the Fort Mills flagpole on Corregidor. The real colors were destroyed by Col. Paul Bunker, a West Point classmate of Douglas MacArthur. After the fall of Bataan, the Japanese moved in artillery and honed in on the target of Corregidor. The island was caught between artillery fire originating from the Cavite and Bataan coasts. The fortress held out until May 6, when Japanese troops invaded the island. Once the Japanese got close enough to threaten Malinta Tunnel, Wainwright sought out the Japanese commander and surrendered the command.

General Wainwright reads the statement ordering all USAFFE troops in the Philippines to surrender. Faced with the execution of his men unless he got all the islands to surrender, Wainwright sent Col. Jesse Traywick to convince the other commanders. Sharp, on Mindanao, had been told to engage in guerrilla warfare by MacArthur and was wary of capitulating without orders. MacArthur gave Sharp the prerogative to make his own decision, but also told Washington he felt Wainwright had become "unbalanced." Another 20,000 troops were surrendered with Wainwright's order.

MacArthur arrives at his office in Melbourne in full uniform. With the command in the Philippines surrendered, he became obsessed with its memory. His headquarters was called Bataan, and it was the word operators at headquarters used to answer the phone. The return to the Philippines dominated MacArthur's thoughts throughout the war, and he could never understand those whose ideas of strategy weren't based on his sacred cause.

This portrait of Pacific Ocean Area commander Adm. Chester Nimitz was a gift to General MacArthur. MacArthur would say that "no finer admiral was ever produced by the United States." He would also call him Admiral "Nee-mitz." In May and June 1942, naval forces under Nimitz's command met the Japanese navy at the battles of the Coral Sea and Midway and sank five Japanese aircraft carriers. Though committed to a "Europe First" strategy, the Combined Chiefs of the United States and Great Britain realized the victories presented the opportunity for a limited offensive in the Pacific.

After the naval victories at Coral Sea and Midway, MacArthur called for an immediate assault on Rabaul. Positioned on the eastern end of the island of New Britain, Rabaul (below) had one of the finest natural harbors in the Pacific, 5 airfields, and over 100,000 Japanese troops by June 1942. MacArthur told Washington to give him ships, planes, and men; he would begin the drive immediately.

Commander in Chief of the U.S. Navy Adm. Ernest J. King was the greatest advocate for offensive warfare in the Pacific. There was no way, however, that King would ever give control of his navy ships to MacArthur for an offensive. He ridiculed the general's proposed drive on Rabaul, favoring a more conservative, limited offensive outlined in plans known as Tasks I–III, issued on July 2, 1942. The objectives were Guadalcanal for the Central and South Pacific areas and Papua New Guinea for the Southwest Pacific area (SWPA).

Port Moresby and its airfields (below) were the keys to control of Papua New Guinea and Northern Australia in 1942. Task II of the Tasks I–III directives was for MacArthur to establish SWPA forces on the north coast of Papua New Guinea. At the time the Allies only had some Australian militia, the Papuan constabulary, and a few engineer troops building airfields at the base at Port Moresby on the southern coast of Papua.

Major General Sutherland stands at the Port Moresby airstrip with Brig. Gen. Robert H. Van Volkenburgh (in pith helmet) and air officer Brig. Gen. Kenneth Walker. MacArthur selected Van Volkenburgh to proceed to Port Moresby with the 40th Antiaircraft Brigade and prepare for Operation PROVIDENCE, the seizure of the north coast of Papua.

Members of the 101st Antiaircraft Artillery man their positions at the heavy bomber airstrip 7 Mile Airdrome in Port Moresby, Papua New Guinea. They were some of the first American combat troops to arrive in Papua New Guinea.

General MacArthur strolls with his air chief, Lt. Gen. George Brett, in Australia during the spring of 1942. By June, airplanes were arriving steadily in SWPA, but MacArthur didn't want Brett to command them; he had no faith in him at all. The War Department agreed to a change and offered MacArthur three different choices for a replacement: Maj. Gen. Frank Andrews, Maj. Gen. James Doolittle, or Maj. Gen. George C. Kenney.

MacArthur arrives in Brisbane, Queensland, Australia, on July 20, 1942. The move put him hundreds of miles closer to Papua, where Australian militia and Papuan constabulary were crossing the 7,000-foot Owen Stanley Mountains scouting for a base on the north coast near Buna Mission. Japanese engineers and infantry of the South Seas Detachment, however, landed at Buna the day after MacArthur arrived in Brisbane.

# CHAPTER 5

# VICTORY AT ALL COST: THE PAPUAN CAMPAIGN
## JULY 1942–JANUARY 1943

On July 21, 1942, the first elements of Maj. Gen. Tomitaro Horii's South Seas Detachment landed at Buna. Under the command of Col. Yosuke Yokoyama, the 15th Engineers and a battalion of the 144th Regiment had a specific purpose: prepare the airstrip at Buna for operations and scout the feasibility of sending a force over the Owen Stanley Mountains to attack Port Moresby, seize its airfields, and dominate Northern Australia. There was no road over the mountains, only the Kokoda Trail, which winds its way over the Owen Stanley Mountains between Buna and Port Moresby. At times just a single-file trek, it was a sheer climb to 7,500 feet where the trail crossed a 5-mile stretch known as "The Gap" to the descending side. Heat, rain, and malaria were the trail's finer qualities. When the Japanese landed at Buna, they faced only the Marouba Force of Australian militia and Papuan constabulary troops under Capt. Herbert Kienzle, which had crossed the Kokoda Trail in June for a reconnaissance to Buna.

A P-39 Airacobra sits on Strip #3 at Milne Bay, Papua New Guinea. In the Philippines MacArthur was forced to learn that air power was the dominant factor on the modern battlefield. The first troops he sent to Papua in April, therefore, were the 96th and 40th Engineers to build airfields. By August there were five bomber and fighter strips at Port Moresby and three at Milne Bay, and airplanes were being sent to inhabit them. What was needed was a commander to guide them, and one had just arrived in Australia.

The arrival of Maj. Gen. George Kenney in August 1942 was the "shot in the arm" MacArthur needed. Kenney found MacArthur despondent and angry with the entire air corps when he arrived in Brisbane. He won his general's confidence by firing five general officers, invigorating his men, and putting planes over Rabaul. A veteran of the First World War and an innovator and inventor, Kenney established Fifth Air Force and became MacArthur's military comrade and confidant during World War II.

On August 26 the Japanese initiated the second half of their pincer movement when the Kure Naval Landing Force, the 362nd Naval Pioneer unit, and a handful of tanks were landed at Milne Bay. In the picture above, Japanese barges are seen beached in Milne Bay after the battle. Luckily, MacArthur realized the danger in early August and forwarded the veteran 18th Brigade, under Brig. Gen. Cyril Clowes, to Milne Bay. Clowes and his force of 4,500 men stopped the Japanese cold and forced them to withdraw on September 6. In the photo below, Australian troops pass one of the knocked-out Japanese tanks.

Brigadier General Clowes (second from right) stands with MacArthur's operations chief, Brig. Gen. Stephen Chamberlin, General Akin, and an unknown officer. Despite handing the Japanese their first defeat on land, Clowes was criticized by MacArthur for failing to send reports to headquarters. MacArthur also felt he moved too cautiously. MacArthur cabled Washington, saying the victory did not reflect the truth of Australian capabilities and crediting his own foresight in sending the 18th Brigade to Milne Bay.

The Japanese had been stopped at Milne Bay, but they were still driving overland on Port Moresby. Major General Horii arrived in Papua on August 14 with 3,000 troops and took personal command of the forces crossing the mountains. Under Horii's command was a unit of volunteers, indigenous tribesmen of Formosa known as the Takasago Unit. By September, Horii's forces were descending the mountains and in sight of the lights of Port Moresby.

MacArthur visits the men of the 32nd Infantry Division during their training at Camp Cable in Queensland, Australia. Maj. Gen. Edward Harding, the division commander, is at right. The 32nd and 41st Divisions were U.S. National Guard units that arrived in Australia the previous spring. Though these troops were raw and untested, the Australians had their hands full in Papua, and MacArthur needed to throw the Americans into the battle as soon as possible.

Moving men and materiel to Papua from Australia was a logistical nightmare. Merchant shipping was scarce, and the U.S. Navy was engaged with the Japanese navy in the battles for Guadalcanal. Major General Kenney came up with a plan to fly everything from Australia to Papua. It had never been done in warfare. The 128th Regiment of the 32nd Infantry Division is shown here loading onto C-47 transports to be ferried to Port Moresby.

Fed by discouraging reports from his staff, MacArthur's assessment of the Australians was not good. He wanted the Japanese stopped and felt he wasn't getting results from the Australian commander in Papua, Maj. Gen. Sidney F. Rowell. Blamey (seen above with MacArthur) felt the heat of MacArthur's displeasure, and on September 23 he went to Port Moresby and relieved Rowell, replacing him with Maj. Gen. Edmund Herring (second from right).

Australian soldiers slog back over the Kokoda Trail, passing an abandoned bicycle left behind during the Japanese advance. Only days after Rowell's relief, an assault by the 25th Brigade on Horii's position at Ioribaiwa found the Japanese gone. Japanese Eighth Area Army command at Rabaul was unable to support the campaigns in Papua and on Guadalcanal simultaneously. Horii was ordered to pull back to the north coast.

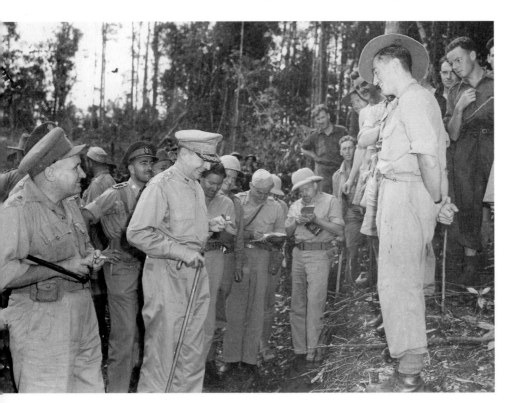

On October 3, MacArthur made his first visit to Port Moresby. Seen at left, he met with troops of the Australian 7th Division and their commander, Maj. Gen. Arthur "Tubby" Allen. Fortunes had turned, and the Australians were pushing the Japanese back to the north coast, but MacArthur remained critical and pressed for speed. Allen questioned MacArthur's criticisms of his Australian troops. MacArthur replied he was just trying to motivate them. Allen told him that was not the way to do it.

Australian troops and their Papuan aides are seen during a rest period on the Kokoda Trail. Though sickly and starving, Horii's troops made a determined defense in the retreat to Buna, and it was a slow process pushing them back over the Owen Stanleys. More Australians found themselves relieved because of the delay. On October 29, Blamey replaced 7th Division commander Allen with Maj. Gen. George Vasey, a veteran of North Africa and Greece who now found himself in the jungles of New Guinea.

Major General Vasey's men reoccupied the village of Kokoda on November 2, driving off Horii's forces. These pictures show the ruins of the village (above) and signposts in Japanese and English standing next to each other in Kokoda (left). Horii's men had almost done the impossible in their epic drive over the Kokoda to take Port Moresby. Now they retreated into the prepared defenses of Buna-Gona-Sanananda. Horii wasn't so lucky; he drowned in the Kumusi River during the retreat.

MacArthur is seen with his commanders at 7 Mile Airdrome at Port Moresby on November 4, 1942, after he arrived by B-17 to set up his advance headquarters. Left to right facing the camera are Lieutenant Colonel Morhouse, antiaircraft officer Brig. Gen. William Marquat, Australian Army Minister F. M. Forde, MacArthur, General Blamey, Lieutenant General Kenney, Lieutenant General Herring, and Brigadier General Walker. MacArthur found it impossible to conduct a war 1,000 miles from the front and decided to move forward.

Soldiers of the 128th Regiment, 32nd Infantry Division, embark on boats of the U.S. Army Small Ships Fleet. The boats transported them up the north coast of Papua for the first American drive against the Japanese defenses at Buna. MacArthur had high hopes for his troops, but the transports were hunted down and raked by Japanese planes on November 16 off the coastal village of Hariko.

The Americans were no better prepared for jungle warfare than anyone else. The conditions were impossible. The Japanese established themselves on the high ground in the coastal areas, maintaining interior lines. The Allies found themselves in the swamps in a marshy land cut by many streams and rivers. For the Australians and Americans it was a two-day trek through the jungle to get from one end of Buna to Sanananda.

The Japanese were established in a network of camouflaged and concealed bunkers with interlocking fields of fire. Capt. Yoshitatsu Yasuda, the senior naval officer, took command in Buna. Col. Yosuke Yokoyama took command of the forces west of the Giruwa River in Gona-Sanananda. In total, over 18,000 Japanese were landed in Papua New Guinea to fight the campaign.

This image captures the essence of the conditions in Papua New Guinea. It was as much a struggle just to live in the muck and mire as it was to fight in it. Malaria ran rampant through the ranks, and sickness and disease claimed more men off the front lines than battle casualties. The 32nd was bogged down before Buna, and soon MacArthur was telling Major General Harding to get his men moving.

Harding addresses his 32nd Infantry "Red Arrow" Division during training camp in Australia. Commanding a National Guard unit from Wisconsin and Michigan, Harding was well liked by all his men and his officers. He deeply felt their suffering, living under such horrendous conditions. MacArthur, always worried that a Japanese victory on Guadalcanal would bring the full might of Japan against him in Papua, relentlessly pushed for speed. On November 22, he ordered Harding to launch an all-out attack "regardless of cost."

In the picture above, Col. Charles Willoughby visits Lt. Gen. Robert Eichelberger and his chief of staff, Brig. Gen. Clovis Byers, in Australia. A West Point graduate and former superintendent of the U.S. Military Academy, Eichelberger was brought to Australia in August 1942 to establish the I Corps headquarters and facilitate the training of the 32nd and 41st Divisions for combat. He was told he would have no part in the Papuan campaign, but in late November MacArthur summoned Eichelberger and Byers to Port Moresby.

Generals Eichelberger and Byers reported to MacArthur in the living room of his headquarters at Port Moresby. MacArthur was angry as he explained that Harding couldn't get the 32nd moving. He said that leadership was what was needed, ordering Eichelberger to the front to ignite the stalled offensive. MacArthur told him, "Take Buna or don't come back alive . . . and that goes for your chief of staff too." Before leaving, Eichelberger saw MacArthur again. He was a different man, telling Eichelberger to watch out for himself as he was no good to anyone dead.

Eichelberger flew over the mountains to the Buna front on December 1, 1942. He found no aggressive spirit at the front line and the rear areas heavy with personnel. In his tour he "chewed out" Harding's officers for the conditions he found. He met with General Harding (above) and told him that he needed to relieve some of his officers to get the division moving. Harding didn't comply, and Eichelberger sacked him and many other commanders. When Harding arrived in Port Moresby, MacArthur said he had no idea why Eichelberger relieved him.

Convinced his drive to liberate the Philippines might end in Papua, at one point MacArthur told Major General Herring that they both would be out of a job if victory wasn't achieved. He was accused of not knowing the conditions in Papua. He believed that Roosevelt and Washington were opposed to him. Many detested MacArthur, yet others had no limit to their admiration for him. Many found him difficult to work with, yet others believed he did everything he could to be cooperative. He was a dichotomy of conflictions and brilliance.

Locked in the struggle for Guadalcanal, the U.S. Navy was not about to risk its ships in the reef-lined waters surrounding Papua New Guinea. MacArthur's Small Ships Fleet was vital to the improvement of conditions at Buna. In the photo above, one of the ships unloads fuel at Hariko. These small ships surveyed the reefs and opened up passageways for larger ships to begin supplying the front by early December.

As soon as airfields north of the mountains could handle the traffic, support by air became a vital element in improving conditions in Papua. In the photo above, a B-17 at Port Moresby is loaded with a 155mm howitzer for transport to the front. Kenney was proving air power was a key element to the campaign. Allied forces began receiving materiel capable of reducing the Japanese bunkers, and the stalled offensive began to move.

Australians of the 7th Division's 21st Brigade fire a mortar on Japanese positions around Gona. The Japanese defenders of Gona fought to the death. On December 9, the Australian 39th Battalion fought its way into the village. They found 800 Japanese dead, many of them used like sandbags in the defenses.

The landing of Brig. Gen. George Wooten's 18th Brigade on the Buna front signaled the beginning of the end of the campaign to take the position. Seen here with Eichelberger in 1943, Wooten was also a veteran of Greece and North Africa, and his brigade proved itself at Milne Bay. The 18th Brigade was brought up the coast by the Small Ships Fleet along with two armor regiments of M3 Stuart light tanks. These armored, tracked vehicles could close with Japanese bunkers and destroy them.

Australians of the 2/6th Armoured Regiment rest beside an M3 Stuart tank the night before the drive on the Buna defenses at Cape Endaiadere southeast of Buna. In the big push of December 24–28, the 18th Brigade and the armor units assaulted the positions held by Col. Hiroshi Yamamoto and men of the 229th Infantry Regiment (left). Though heavy in casualties, the movement allowed the Australians to flank the Japanese defenses at both the old and new airstrips.

The Japanese defensive positions at the Triangle in the southwest and the old and new airstrips to the southeast had to be seized to take Buna. Both positions were a vast network of bunkers, interwoven networks of machine-gun fire, and trenches. They were finally seized at the end of December by American and Australian troops. Eichelberger (above center), a true front-line commander, is seen at the Triangle after its capture.

Engineers repair a bridge between the old and new Buna airstrips.

Scenes of the battlefield for the Buna airstrips.

Soldiers of the 32nd Infantry Division's 128th Regiment fire on Japanese positions at Cape Endaiadere. On January 1, 1943, three companies of the 128th moved with the 18th Brigade and tanks of the 2/12 Armor Battalion, pushing through the old airstrip and seizing Giropa Point. Resistance in Buna ceased the next day.

Over 1,500 dead Japanese were found in the defenses of Buna. The commanders, Colonel Yamamoto and Imperial Japanese navy captain Yasuda, fought to the end and then committed suicide. Many troops tried to get out by water. In the photo above, Australian and American troops inspect an unfortunate Japanese landing craft and its occupants.

Generals Eichelberger and Blamey tour Buna after its fall. The battle had been a costly lesson in jungle warfare. The Australians suffered 267 dead and 1,400 wounded in the battle. The Americans suffered over 2,400 casualties, with 353 dead. Victory was achieved at Buna, but it was a heavy price to pay.

On Christmas Day 1942 MacArthur posed for cameras outside his headquarters at Port Moresby. He is wearing the leather A2 jacket given to him by George Kenney. He wore it throughout World War II and beyond. MacArthur pushed his commanders and men to the brink, and to victory. He was appalled at the cost. Another way of prosecuting this war in the Pacific had to be found. He would proclaim victory to an eager press, but he would also say, "No more Bunas."

The campaign wasn't over with the fall of Buna. The Japanese force defending Sanananda Point and the vicinity (shown above) still held strong with three battalions of the 41st Infantry Regiment, veterans of the Kokoda Trail. Maj. Gen. Kensaku Oda arrived on December 13 to take command of the South Seas Detachment and defend Sanananda to the finish.

Generals Eichelberger and Herring, seen above during the Sanananda campaign in January 1943, were a good example of Allied cooperation. MacArthur and Blamey had a jealous streak over whose troops were better, but Wooten and Eichelberger were quick to help each other when necessary. Australian and American forces joined together in the reduction of Sanananda.

Men of the 163rd Regiment, 41st Infantry Division, make their way to the front at Sanananda on January 2, 1943. They are in crisp uniforms and carry M1 Garand rifles. The .30-caliber Garand rifle was the first semiautomatic rifle issued by the U.S. Army and a favorite of the men. Along with men from the 32nd Division's 127th Regiment and Wooten's 18th Brigade, the men of the 163rd took Sanananda.

A 37mm artillery piece is fired in support of the Australian-American drive on Sanananda. The 37mm gun M3 was the first U.S. antitank weapon in World War II. German armor made it obsolete in Europe by 1943, but it was used until 1945 in the Pacific. It was a weapon that could be towed by a jeep and fired as support for infantry. This crew is working astride the Giruwa River. Japanese resistance ended in Sanananda on January 22.

As did Yasuda and Yamamoto at Buna, General Oda committed suicide with the fall of Sanananda. Many of the Australian and American wounded were buried at Sanananda Cemetery. Here an American visits the grave of his officer, Lt. H. R. Fisk, who died during the battle on January 9. In the entirety of the campaign, only 3,400 of the 18,000 Japanese who landed in Papua survived. The Australians and Americans suffered 8,335 total casualties, with 2,037 Australian and 835 American dead.

The campaign ended in victory, but it was still an uncertain future for the Allies. The Japanese remained strong and on the offensive. Eichelberger was hailed by the press as the victor of Papua New Guinea, but he too had come close to being relieved by MacArthur. Eichelberger saw a future as a battlefield commander, but would not see the front again for another year. MacArthur had his own ideas for the future.

Grateful for victory in Papua, MacArthur and Prime Minister Curtin knew the
Southwest Pacific Area needed more support to go on the offensive while
Japanese forces were off balance. When the Combined Chiefs met at Casablanca
in January 1943, Curtin sent messages to his fellow world leaders pleading for
support. The European effort maintained precedence, but it was agreed at
Casablanca to continue to support the limited offensive toward Rabaul.

Though defeated in Papua and Guadalcanal, the Japanese were moving in the Huon Gulf region of New Guinea. Three thousand 51st Division troops moved from Lae to Wau to capture the airstrip there. Held by the Australian Kanga Force, General Kenney (left) flew the 17th Brigade into Wau and stopped the Japanese on January 28, 1943. Japanese Eighth Area Army command decided to reinforce Lae with 6,900 more troops of the 51st Division. U.S. Navy code breakers predicted a March convoy from Rabaul to Lae.

Armed with this vital intelligence, Kenney worked out an operational plan to hit the convoy. For months he had been training his pilots for low-level attacks on shipping. American and Australian pilots geared up for the Battle of the Bismarck Sea (below). In the attacks of March 2–4, Japan lost 8 transports, 4 destroyers, and 3,000 men. Japan would never again use a large convoy to try to reinforce New Guinea.

One transport burns, and medium bombers strafe a second transport (bottom).

After the victory MacArthur submitted his
ELKTON III plan to Washington. Simultaneous
drives by MacArthur's and Adm. William F.
Halsey's forces would culminate in the destruction
of Rabaul. Resources were not available to take
Rabaul, but the dual drive was approved. Halsey
arrived at MacArthur's headquarters in Brisbane
on April 14 (above), and they agreed to a series of
landings known as CARTWHEEL. Halsey and
MacArthur immediately liked each other,
embarking on a lifelong friendship.

In January 1943 MacArthur requested the services
of Lt. Gen. Walter Krueger. Krueger arrived in
February with the newly constituted Sixth Army
headquarters. A year younger than MacArthur,
they shared the same birthday. He was old, but
MacArthur was too. Enlisting in the army in 1898
as a private, Krueger rose to the rank of general.
He was nobody's "yes man" and was the perfect
balance of caution and capability for MacArthur's
boldness.

MacArthur sits on a table at a press conference in early 1943. The general's catering to the press was calculated: It generated support among the public for his campaigns. It also caused most of the animosity from the Navy, and Washington often questioned MacArthur's release of certain information and the viability of his facts. After the Bismarck Sea battle, MacArthur's figures on Japanese losses were inflated compared to those of Washington.

As commander in chief of SWPA, MacArthur had no control of troops under Allied Land Forces commander General Blamey. He could only suggest things to him. However, MacArthur could create and control his own task forces. He created ALAMO Force, consisting of all the American units in the theater under the command of General Krueger. Krueger became the second part to the team being created. MacArthur had his airman in Kenney; now he had his infantryman in Krueger.

Krueger's arrival was a slap in the face for Robert Eichelberger. He was the victor at Buna. Didn't he deserve the command of ALAMO Force? Eichelberger requested a transfer, but MacArthur said he needed him. Eichelberger loved press and publicity as much as MacArthur did, but he would not get much training troops as a subordinate to Krueger. Here, Krueger decorates Eichelberger with the Legion of Merit.

Australian troops go through the Jungle Training Center at Canundra, Australia. May's TRIDENT conference in Washington authorized sending the 24th Infantry and 1st Cavalry Divisions to MacArthur. Eichelberger became responsible for training the 24th. At Canundra all the lessons from Papua were incorporated into the course. Jungle-infested areas were the future in the Southwest Pacific, and lucky was the man who got extensive training before CARTWHEEL began.

The greatest gift the U.S. Navy ever gave MacArthur was Rear Adm. Daniel Barbey. He was the amphibious genius of World War II and just the man MacArthur needed for the upcoming CARTWHEEL operations. Arriving in January 1943, Barbey established the VII Amphibious Force with few staff members and even fewer ships. Barbey's accumulation of ships began immediately.

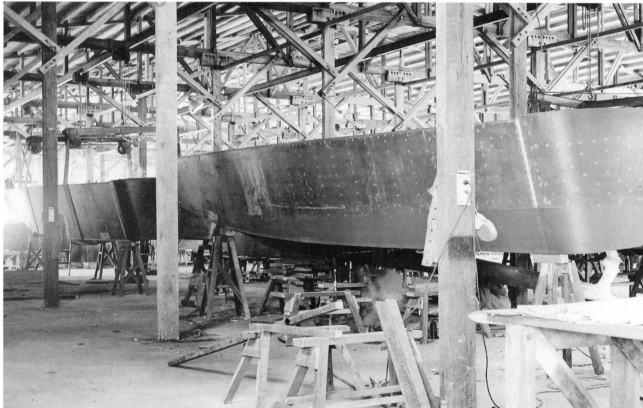

Preparations had been made for amphibious war. Training centers like the one at Toorbul Point (top) had been set up in Australia the previous September. Most importantly, Barbey was getting an army special engineer brigade, trained in Massachusetts for boat and shore operations. At Cairns, Australia, a factory was in operation creating another wonder weapon of World War II, the Higgins boat, which could drive right up onto a beach and quickly be unloaded.

The lack of shipping worldwide was a major problem for the Allies. It was the reason for the delay between the directive and actual CARTWHEEL operations. Once Barbey felt he had enough ships, operations would begin.

The Landing Craft, Vehicle (LCV) was the most common boat created by the Andrew Higgins boat company in New Orleans. It could carry a jeep or a platoon of thirty-six men.

The Landing Craft, Mechanized (LCM) was a British invention that could carry over 120,000 pounds.

The Landing Ship, Tank (LST) was also a British invention. It too could advance right to the beach and discharge tons of vehicles and materiel and hundreds of personnel.

An amphibious Landing Vehicle, Tracked (LVT) Alligator sits in front of its host ship, the Landing Ship, Dock (LSD), which could flood its decks to discharge the LVTs.

CARTWHEEL began with the invasion of Kiriwina and Woodlark in the Trobriand Islands with the CHRONICLE Task Force. The islands provided the air bases needed to support Halsey's drive up the Solomon Islands. On June 30, Barbey's fleet put the 112th Regimental Combat Team (RCT) on Woodlark and the 158th Infantry on Kiriwina. In the photo at right, ALAMO commander Krueger welcomes MacArthur to Kiriwina.

The same day as the CHRONICLE landings, the 162nd Infantry Regiment went ashore at Nassau Bay on the coast of New Guinea. MacArthur's next targets were the harbor and airfield at Lae. Nassau Bay was needed as a supply depot for that assault. Barbey used PT boats to land the troops, and by July 4 he had 1,400 ashore. A 105mm howitzer of the 205th Field Artillery (below) is concealed for action in Nassau Bay.

Japan planned a counterthrust to CARTWHEEL and moved Fourth Air Army units into airfields at Wewak, New Guinea, and Rabaul. Code breakers were picking up signals of the movement. Kenney had a secret air base built at Tsili Tsili, far enough forward to base fighter planes to cover the longer range: heavy B-17 and B-24 and medium B-25 bombers. On August 17–18, 1943, Kenney's airmen raided Wewak (above), destroying nearly 100 planes on the ground. It was a major turn in the air war just before the assault on Lae.

President Roosevelt's wife, Eleanor, visited the Pacific and came to Australia in September 1943. MacArthur did not meet her, citing the operations against Salamaua and Lae. Here, Jean MacArthur greets Mrs. Roosevelt upon her arrival at Eagle Farm Airdrome in Brisbane. MacArthur was opposed to Roosevelt politically, and his name was already being spoken of as a presidential candidate for the 1944 election.

Lae had a harbor and good airstrip (shown above) and was the launch point into the Ramu and Markham Valleys that traversed New Guinea for 400 miles to the west. Advancing land-based air power negated the need for U.S. Navy carrier-based airplanes to cover MacArthur's amphibious moves. Airplanes out of Lae would cover the entire Huon Peninsula, the next objective of CARTWHEEL. On September 4, Major General Wooten's veteran 9th Division landed east of Lae.

MacArthur was putting Lae and the neighboring Japanese strongpoint of Salamaua in a vise. The day after the landings at Lae, paratroopers of the 503rd Parachute Infantry were dropped to grab the airstrip at Nadzab, west of Lae. In the picture at left, MacArthur talks with the paratroopers at 7 Mile Airdrome before the mission. Kenney put 96 C-47 cargo planes in the air with over 200 bombers and fighters to drop the 503rd.

MacArthur flew in the B-17 *Talisman* to watch the parachute drop over Nadzab. When Kenney warned him against it, MacArthur said the only thing he was worried about was throwing up "in front of the kids." After the airstrip was captured, Kenney flew in the Australian 7th Division's 25th Brigade.

Members of the 503rd and the 25th Brigade shake hands at the airstrip in the picture at right.

Lt. Gen. Hidemitsu Nakano's 51st Division in Lae was nearly surrounded, with the 9th Division's 24th Brigade on one side and the 7th Division's 25th Brigade on the other. American and Australian troops were also pushing north from Nassau Bay toward Salamaua. Eleven thousand Japanese fled westward through the jungle. On September 15 Lae fell, and Nakano was found among the smoldering ruins (left), another suicide victim.

After the victory at Lae, MacArthur immediately wanted Finschhafen at the eastern end of the Huon Peninsula. Basically an overnight operation, Barbey's ships brought the 9th Division's 20th Brigade to Finschhafen. Intelligence chief Willoughby estimated there were only 350 Japanese there. The Australians found thousands that were soon joined by the Japanese 20th Division. It took reinforcements and two months of intense fighting to secure the area.

The CARTWHEEL drive could not move fast enough for MacArthur. Finschhafen, like Buna, showed how his push for speed put the burden on his troops. Always on MacArthur's mind were the Philippines, advancing the timetable of operations and moving him forward. In August 1943 at Quebec's Quadrant Conference, however, the Combined Chiefs discussed ending MacArthur's drive in New Guinea. He had to prove that the New Guinea–Philippine axis to Japan was the most economical in time and lives. He wasn't doing it.

Kenney's Fifth Air Force now had the forward fighter bases to cover massive bombing raids on Rabaul. In the top photo, a B-25 Mitchell bomber of the 38th Bomb Group comes in low over the ships in Simpson Harbor. Phosphorous bombs are dropped over the facilities at Rabaul in the bottom photo. In November 1943 a Japanese cruiser force intending to oppose Halsey's invasion at Empress Augusta Bay was destroyed at Rabaul by U.S. Navy carrier planes.

MacArthur now looked to the Vitiaz Straits between New Britain and New Guinea. He called upon Maj. Gen. William Rupertus's (below) 1st Marine Division to seize Cape Gloucester on western New Britain. Marine planners rejected the ALAMO headquarters plan. MacArthur listened to their complaints (left), and then told General Krueger to work it out with them. He told Rupertus, "I know what the Marines think of me, but I also know that when they go in to a fight they can be counted on to do an outstanding job."

General MacArthur quit wearing medals and ribbons in 1943. This is how his blouse would have been arranged at the time of his death in 1964.

MacArthur's iconic hat was created in Manila while he was military advisor to the Philippine Commonwealth in the 1930s. He wore it up until his death. During the Occupation of Japan, the top was wearing through. MacArthur's wife, Jean, had it re-covered with one of the general's khaki shirts when he was sick for a few days in 1948.

In December 1944, Douglas MacArthur was promoted to a five-star General of the Army along with George C. Marshall, Dwight D. Eisenhower, and Henry Arnold. Admirals Ernest King, Chester Nimitz, and William Leahy were made five-star Fleet Admirals of the U.S. Navy at the same time. All of them wore the same style insignia.

The Japanese created currency for all the territories of their conquests. These are examples of the money that replaced the Philippine peso. It was referred to as "Mickey Mouse" currency by the Filipinos. The intelligence section of MacArthur's headquarters counterfeited the currency and flooded the islands with it between 1943–44; by 1945 it was nearly worthless.

General MacArthur is captured in this photo (see also page 103) taken on Christmas Day 1942 on the grounds of his headquarters at Port Moresby, Papua New Guinea. He wears the leather A2 jacket given to him by his air chief, Lt. Gen. George Kenney. MacArthur wore the jacket throughout World War II and in the early days of the Korean War until he acquired a new one.

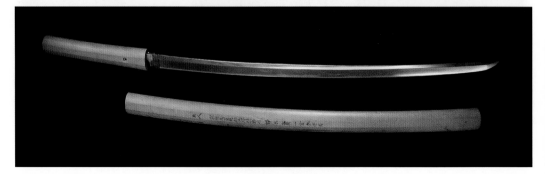

One of four Waterman fountain pens MacArthur used to sign the surrender documents on the USS *Missouri* in Tokyo Bay on September 2, 1945. MacArthur used a total of six pens to sign the documents. One Waterman was given to General Wainwright and is now at the West Point Museum; another was given to British general Arthur Percival and is at the Cheshire Military Museum in England. The two others are at the MacArthur Memorial. MacArthur also used a pen that belonged to Col. Courtney Whitney and resides with the Whitney family. The sixth pen was Jean MacArthur's orange Parker Duofold; it was stolen from her apartment in New York in the 1980s.

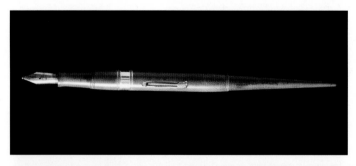

On October 20, 1944, General MacArthur delivered his "I Have Returned" speech on the beach at Palo, Leyte, for broadcast via radio. He used this microphone provided by the U.S. Army Signal Corps. After the broadcast, the microphone was tucked away by CBS newsman Bill Dunn.

Douglas MacArthur's gold baton signifying his rank as a field marshal of the Philippine Islands was given to him by President Manuel Quezon in August 1936. It was one of the few personal items Jean MacArthur grabbed before leaving the Manila Hotel for Corregidor on Christmas Eve 1941. Everything else the MacArthurs owned was left in the hotel, only to be destroyed in 1945.

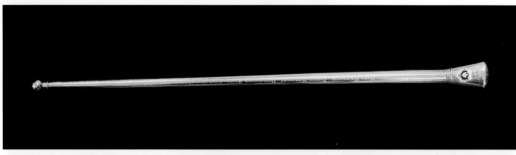

Japanese general Hideki Tojo's sword was given to Douglas MacArthur by Lt. Gen. Robert Eichelberger in 1945. Eichelberger obtained the sword after General Tojo attempted suicide. It hangs in the MacArthur Memorial in Norfolk, Virginia.

The Distinguished Service Cross is the second highest award with which the U.S. Army decorates its soldiers. MacArthur was awarded three of them during his career. The first two were bestowed upon him for his service on the fields of France in the First World War. The third was awarded for action during the drive to Manila in 1945.

The front and reverse of Douglas MacArthur's Medal of Honor are shown at right. The caption on the reverse reads: "The Congress to General Douglas MacArthur, US Army, Bataan Peninsula, DEC 1941–MAR 42." MacArthur was awarded the Medal of Honor in March 1942 for service in the Philippine Campaign. The Allies needed a hero, and Roosevelt wanted no opportunity overlooked to give the award to MacArthur. At the time it was awarded, MacArthur and his father became the only father-son pair to hold the medal.

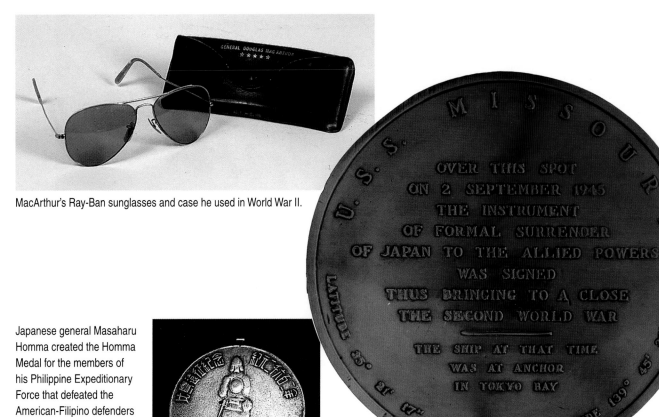

MacArthur's Ray-Ban sunglasses and case he used in World War II.

Japanese general Masaharu Homma created the Homma Medal for the members of his Philippine Expeditionary Force that defeated the American-Filipino defenders of the Philippines in 1942. The image of the Japanese soldier was stamped on a Philippine peso.

A plaque on the starboard deck of the USS *Missouri* marks the spot where the surrender of Japan took place on September 2, 1945.

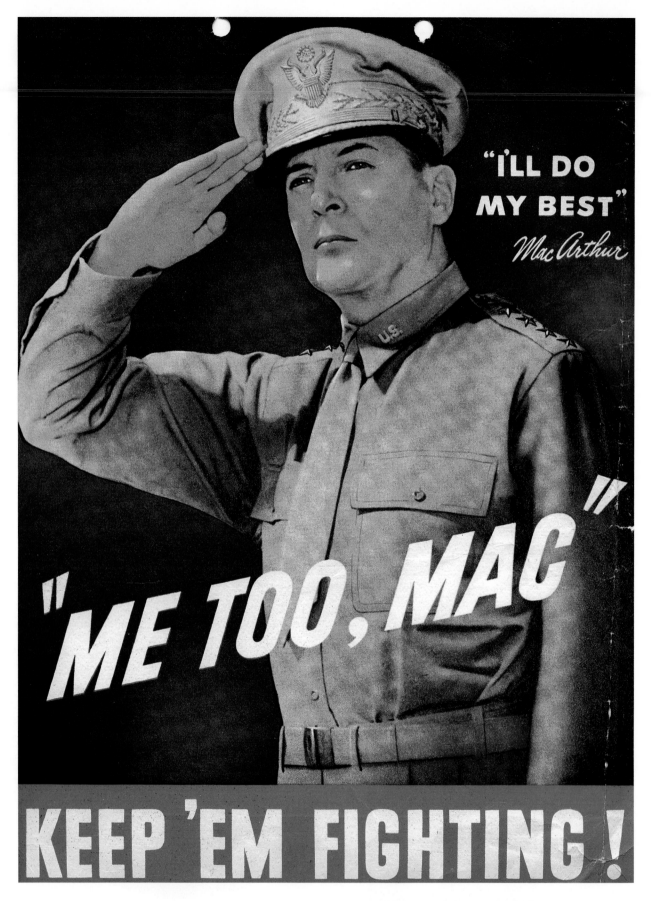

"I'LL DO MY BEST" *MacArthur*

"ME TOO, MAC"

KEEP 'EM FIGHTING !

Douglas MacArthur became an icon of the Allied cause at the beginning of World War II. At a time when the Allied Powers were retreating on all fronts, the heroic defense of the Philippines left a lasting impression upon the American public. MacArthur's slogan, "I'll do my best," was used in all types of media. It was all that could be hoped of everyone at a desperate time.

In August 1943, Lt. Cmdr. Charles "Chick" Parsons came up with the idea of printing Philippine and American flags and the MacArthur slogan "I Shall Return" on a host of items and then inserting them by submarine into the guerrilla areas of the Philippines. When Colonel Whitney proposed the idea to MacArthur, the general wrote on the memorandum, "No Objection . . . I Shall Return!" Cigarettes, matches, sewing needle kits, candy, gum, pencils—everything was emblazoned and funneled into the islands. The presence of the items in the occupied Philippines thrilled the populace and enraged the Japanese.

General of the Army Douglas MacArthur, Supreme Commander of the Allied Powers, salutes on the reviewing stand of the Independence Day Parade, July 4, 1949 (see also page 198). Each year, the occupying forces held the Independence Day Parade on the Imperial Palace Plaza in Tokyo, Japan. British Commonwealth Occupation Force commander Lt. Gen. H.C.H. Robertson is on the left in the background, and the commander of the Far East Air Forces, Lt. Gen. Edward Stratemeyer, is on the right in the background.

Philippine painter Antonio García Llamas's 1946 portrait of General of the Army Douglas MacArthur.

The MacArthur Memorial is the final resting place of General of the Army Douglas MacArthur and his wife, Jean. In 1960 the City of Norfolk offered MacArthur its 1850 City Hall building to house a museum containing all of his memorabilia and papers. MacArthur agreed on the condition that he and his wife could be buried there. The memorial now serves as a museum, research, and educational center.

As a diversion from the landing at Cape Gloucester, the 112th RCT and the 148th Field Artillery were put ashore at Arawe, south of the main target. On December 15 over 1,000 men of the DIRECTOR Task Force were put ashore. The landing prompted intense Japanese air attacks and a counterattack on land. Eventually the 158th "Bushmasters" (above) were brought in with the 1st Marine Tank Regiment to end the fighting on January 6.

The 112th RCT was a Texas National Guard unit. Here Texans of the unit pose with their state flag. The men hold captured Japanese Type 99 rifles, the standard infantry rifle for the Japanese military.

Vice Adm. Thomas C. Kinkaid arrived in the Southwest Pacific on November 26 as its new 7th Fleet Commander. There were two previous commanders of the 7th Fleet and MacArthur had faith in neither. He felt they made no effort in the Papuan or CARTWHEEL campaigns to get the fleet to work at full capacity. Kinkaid was different. Like Krueger and Kenney, he was a free thinker who could put MacArthur's ideas into conceptual plans. He was the final piece in MacArthur's team of leaders.

Army Chief of Staff Gen. George C. Marshall made his only visit to MacArthur's theater on December 14, 1943. Marshall was returning to Washington from the Middle East and wanted to relay the decisions from the Cairo and Tehran conferences. The Combined Chiefs favored a Central Pacific drive at Japan. In the picture below, a junior officer seems to have drawn the displeasure of General Kenney in front of Chamberlin, Krueger, MacArthur, and Marshall.

Major General Rupertus's DEXTERITY force went ashore at Cape Gloucester on December 26. The Marines seized the airstrip but got sucked into a fight in the jungle with the Japanese 17th Division. As at Arawe, the Japanese were finally decimated and retreated across the island to Rabaul, where they waited for the assault that never came.

LSTs discharge troops of the 32nd Division at Saidor on January 2, 1944. The invasion triggered the most fortunate incident of MacArthur's campaigns in the Pacific. The landing forced the Japanese 20th Division to vacate Sio or risk encirclement by Australians driving through the Ramu Valley. Australian minesweepers clearing Sio found the 20th Division's codebooks. Soon they were in the hands of MacArthur's code breakers in Brisbane, the secret group known as Central Bureau.

Armed with the 20th Division's codebooks, General Akin's (center) code breakers at Central Bureau began decrypting hundreds of Japanese messages each day. The new intelligence gave MacArthur the layout of Japanese strengths throughout his theater. Hansa Bay was the next operation for CARTWHEEL, but Central Bureau revealed it was heavily defended. Hollandia, by contrast, was not. To make the move to Hollandia and bypass Hansa Bay, acquiring a jump-off base in the Admiralty Islands became a necessity. Second to the left of Akin is Col. Joe Sherr. He never saw the big break in code breaking, having been killed in an air crash over India in October 1943.

Fifth Air Force fighter and bomber commanders Brig. Gen. Paul Wurtsmith and Maj. Gen. Ennis Whitehead (left) began hitting the Admiralties. Whitehead's pilots said they were getting no resistance and seeing no activity. With Whitehead's information, Kenney proposed an invasion to General MacArthur, saying the seizure of the Admiralties would isolate and neutralize Rabaul. Through Central Bureau's code breakers, MacArthur knew there were 4,000 Japanese in the islands, but grabbing them would put the "cork in the bottle" in relation to Rabaul.

Admiral Kinkaid was for the gamble, but Krueger and Barbey hated the idea. Krueger was planning on using the entire 1st Cavalry Division on the scheduled invasion date months away. Now he was told only a 1,000-man reconnaissance in force would be sent in. MacArthur said he would go along to make the decision to bring in support or withdraw the force. In the photo at right, MacArthur and Kinkaid fly from Australia to Goodenough Island to board the light cruiser USS *Phoenix* for the invasion.

The Admiralties have two main islands, Manus and Los Negros, which form the basin of Seeadler Harbor. The Japanese expected the assault on the wide beaches of the harbor. It was the obvious choice, so on February 27, 1,000 men of the 2nd Squadron, 5th Cavalry (above), landed at Hyane Harbor on Los Negros, throwing Japanese defenses into confusion.

MacArthur and Kinkaid view the pre-invasion bombardment of Los Negros Island from the bridge of the USS *Phoenix* on February 27, 1944. It was MacArthur's first extended cruise on a U.S. Navy vessel. He was amazed at the capability of naval firepower to silence the opposition on Los Negros. Kinkaid said MacArthur was a firm believer in naval firepower thereafter.

A few hours after the landings, MacArthur visited the beaches with Kinkaid and his aide, Col. Roger Egeberg (above). He toured the field and was in the open at all times, thoroughly dispelling any of the cavalrymen's notions of "Dugout Doug." As he was leaving the island, he congratulated and decorated Lt. Marvin Henshaw, the first officer on shore, with the Distinguished Service Cross (right).

MacArthur embraces the task force commander, Brig, Gen. William Chase, before leaving Los Negros. He told him, "You have your teeth in them. Don't let go." MacArthur ordered in the reinforcements, but Chase and his men had a few rough nights before they arrived. Over the next few weeks the entire 1st Cavalry Division was put ashore. It took another month and a half to end the fighting, but the capture of the Admiralties guaranteed MacArthur's dream of returning to the Philippines.

The landing in the Admiralties astounded the Combined Chiefs. MacArthur immediately submitted his RENO IV plan, which aimed at crossing New Guinea and hitting the Philippines in early 1945. It was approved. Here MacArthur wears the sash of a Knights Commander of the Order of the Bath, one of the highest decorations the British government can bestow. It was awarded on March 17; that night MacArthur addressed the Australian Parliament and repeated his pledge to return to the Philippines. It was a statement made in confidence.

# CHAPTER 7

# RENO IV OPERATIONS ACROSS NEW GUINEA
## APRIL–SEPTEMBER 1944

At a 1st Cavalry burial service on Los Negros Island, division commander Maj. Gen. Innis P. Swift stands hatless at the graveside while everyone else wears helmets. Their victory in the Admiralties created the opportunity for another bold strike, but Japan's Second Area Army based in Davao, Philippines, was moving reinforcements into western New Guinea. As in Papua and CARTWHEEL, in the RENO IV operations MacArthur's mantra was speed, and the first target was Hollandia.

Col. Bonner Fellers, an officer in the Operations section of headquarters, presented MacArthur with the idea of hitting Hollandia, 580 miles west of Saidor. He did so behind the back of his capable and competent chief, Major General Chamberlin. Chamberlin fired Fellers, but MacArthur bought the idea, code-named Operation RECKLESS. It was an ironic name, considering the jump to Hollandia was made with full confidence due to intelligence provided by code breaking. The operation bypassed Lt. Gen. Hatazo Adachi's 40,000 troops of the Eighteenth Army at the original target of Hansa Bay.

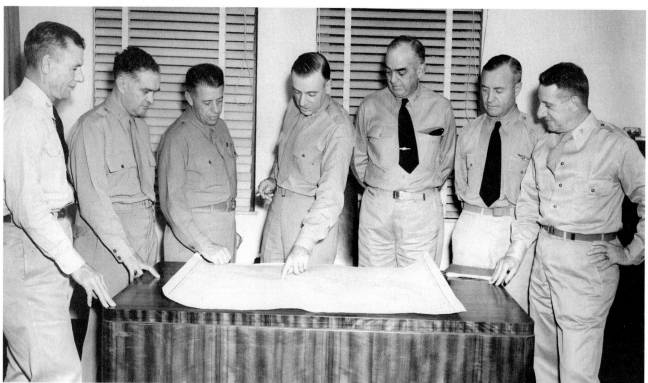

The staffs of General MacArthur and Admiral Nimitz are shown in Brisbane, Australia, on March 26, 1944; left to right are Captain Grew, Marshall, Kenney, Sutherland, Kinkaid, Vice Adm. Forrest Sherman, and Chamberlin. Under directive to support MacArthur's jump to Hollandia, the Navy was going to provide air cover for the invasion. Nimitz and his staff arrived in Brisbane on the 25th and found MacArthur and his staff at the dock waiting to greet them.

MacArthur and Nimitz pose for photographers during the Brisbane Conference. Just seeing each other went a long way in ensuring cooperation, and the conference was cordial and beneficial. Nimitz's greatest fear about the operation was Japanese land-based air power and the threat it posed to his aircraft carriers. General Kenney, benefitting from the intelligence code breaking was providing, knew all the Japanese air assets and promised they would be eliminated by the time of the invasion.

The Japanese believed their airplanes were safe at Hollandia, out of range of the Fifth Air Force. Unknown to them, however, was that P-38 Lightning fighter planes were now outfitted with wing tanks for extra fuel. In raids at the end of March, Kenney's bombers destroyed Japanese air power at Wewak and Hollandia. The image above shows parachute bombs falling on Hollandia. The Japanese were isolated as anything on the water was obliterated, like the barges at Hansa Bay in the photo on the next page.

Barbey, MacArthur, Kenney, and Krueger are caught by the cameraman in December 1943. They were becoming experts in the joint use of land, air, and naval forces in a military campaign. At Hollandia they planned three landings at once. Hollandia's airfields were 10 miles inland from the shore, between Humboldt and Tanahmerah Bays. Eichelberger's I Corps, consisting of the 24th and 41st Divisions, landed in the bays, and a third force, Brig. Gen. Jens Doe's 163rd RCT, went ashore at Aitape, east of Hollandia, to put up a flank guard and seize the Tadji Airdrome.

MacArthur was now pushing out of Northeast New Guinea and into Netherlands New Guinea. Papua and Northeast New Guinea were Australian mandates since the end of the First World War, and Australia had laws about its conscripted men serving outside Australian territory. The campaign into Netherlands New Guinea was to be an American show, and General Krueger's ALAMO Force became what was intended all along: Sixth Army.

MacArthur strides the deck of the light cruiser USS *Nashville* after boarding the ship at Finschhafen. The *Nashville* traveled north to Cape Gloucester, where MacArthur visited the officers and men of the 1st Marine Division, soon to go back under the control of Admiral Nimitz. The invasion convoy then journeyed north of the Admiralties as a ruse before heading southwest to the Hollandia coast.

An LST loaded with troops and tons of supplies keeps its position in the convoy headed to Hollandia. Three task forces were en route, one having come all the way from Goodenough Island, nearly 1,000 miles from Hollandia. Gathering the fleet at the recently acquired Manus Island in the Admiralties, Barbey had over 80,000 men embarked on 217 ships. Such numbers were unheard of in the previous year. Industrial capability was in overdrive in the United States, the arsenal of democracy.

Shells are strewn on the deck of the USS *Nashville* as its 6-inch guns hammer the coastline at Humboldt Bay on April 22. Barbey had control of the amphibious force at Humboldt Bay, and Rear Adm. William Fechteler commanded the force at Tanahmerah Bay; they were separated by 30 miles of coastline. There were 11,000 Japanese troops in the area, but they were mostly service troops and evaporated before the onslaught.

Supplies began stacking up on the beaches, and soldiers had to pitch in to help with the unloading. At Tanahmerah Bay, intelligence that swamps were just beyond the beach had been ignored. Men and materiel had to find a way across. MacArthur was very lucky, though forewarned by code breaking, that no one was there. On the night of April 23 a lone Japanese bomber made a night run and planted a bomb amidst the stacked supplies, causing a monstrous explosion.

Maj. Gen. Horace Fuller took command ashore at Humboldt Bay while his 162nd Infantry Regiment (right) began pushing inland against little opposition. Hollandia's four airfields were located on Lake Sentani, equidistant between Humboldt and Tanahmerah Bays. The 41st and 24th Divisions pushed inward, pinching the airbases between them. The maneuver was completed by April 26. Over 340 wrecked aircraft were found on the airstrips at Hollandia.

Four hours after the first wave went ashore, MacArthur landed in Fuller's area at Humboldt Bay. Here he is seen flanked on the left by his naval aide, Capt. Felix Johnson, and his aides Colonels Roger Egeberg and Lloyd Lehrbas, with Fuller grabbing his arm. MacArthur and Fuller were also joined by Krueger and Eichelberger. MacArthur walked the beaches for 3 miles and amazed Eichelberger by not sweating a drop.

Once back aboard the USS *Nashville*, MacArthur had the ship head for Tanahmerah Bay. At 4:00 PM, he visited Maj. Gen. Frederick Irving's sector. In the photo above, he shakes Irving's hand while hundreds of 24th Division soldiers and I Corps commander Lieutenant General Eichelberger (background center) look on. The Hollandia operation was a complete success, resulting in 3,000 Japanese dead and 7,000 more chased off into the jungle at a cost of 150 American lives.

MacArthur strikes a confident pose during his visit to Aitape on April 23. Brigadier General Doe's PERSECUTION Task Force quickly grabbed the Tadji Airdrome. Aitape's airstrips were needed because Nimitz would not let his carriers stay in the Hollandia area, fearful of Japanese land-based air power. The position at Aitape also placed a buffer between the airdrome at Hollandia and Adachi's 40,000 Japanese bypassed at Hansa Bay.

Within days of the landing at Aitape, P-38 Lightning fighters were already based there, making Nimitz's aircraft carriers unnecessary.

Col. Leif Sverdrup was perhaps the key engineer officer in the Southwest Pacific. In a war that depended on advancing land-based air power, it was Sverdrup who scouted out airstrips and then oversaw engineers resurfacing old ones, carving new ones out of the jungle, and transforming coral atolls into airdromes.

Hollandia was turned into a city of over 140,000 people. Headquarters moved forward from Brisbane to the complex at Lake Sentani, below the beautiful Cyclops Mountains. Engineers built a facility to serve as MacArthur's residence and headquarters (above) on top of Engineer Hill overlooking the lake. American journalists said MacArthur had a mansion built for himself at Hollandia, but he only stayed there a total of four nights.

Engineers working on the air base at Hollandia soon realized that only a few of the old Japanese strips could handle the weight of the B-17 Flying Fortress and the B-24 Liberator. It would take longer to convert the other fields. MacArthur needed strips to accommodate the heavy bombers that would cover his drive to the Vogelkop Peninsula at the western end of New Guinea. Wakde Island (right) was 140 miles west of Hollandia and had a coral base strong enough to handle anything. It was the next target.

Wakde Island was very small and rested just off the coast of New Guinea. The airstrip took up practically the whole island, and not everything that needed to be landed on Wakde would fit, so the initial invasion was made at Arara, New Guinea, on May 15. Once again Doe's 163rd RCT was the strike force. In the photo above, a line of M4 Sherman tanks has just been discharged on the beach at Arara by LST 457.

On the beach at Wakde, stretcher-bearers run off their LCVP landing craft under hostile fire. There were 800 Japanese on Wakde who had built a defense system of concrete pillboxes on the island. It was a combat landing, and it took two days to eliminate resistance. All but four of the Japanese fought to the death. The 163rd had over 100 casualties, but Wakde became a key base and soon had two heavy bomber and two fighter squadrons in operation.

Just west of Arara were Maffin Bay and the village of Sarmi. Home to Lt. Gen. Tagami Hachiro's 36th Division, the area was needed for staging future operations, and General Krueger had to take it. Here, the 278th Field Artillery initiates the campaign on May 25, firing their 155mm howitzers at Japanese positions. The Japanese manned their prepared defenses at Lone Tree Hill and sucked the 158th RCT and then the 6th Division's 20th Infantry Regiment into a months-long battle. There were 400 American dead before the last of the 4,000 Japanese were defeated, but Maffin Bay (left) was the staging area for five future operations.

The prize for MacArthur's drive across Netherlands New Guinea was the island of Biak. Part of the Schouten Islands, it had three Japanese airdromes capable of handling groups of heavy bombers. MacArthur promised Nimitz air support for his moves into the Marianas and Palaus in the near future, and Biak was in range to provide that support. MacArthur coveted the island, as did the Japanese—Col. Naoyuki Kuzumi and his 11,000 defenders were waiting for the Americans. Now a veteran unit, the 162nd Regiment was landed on Biak by LSTs (right) on May 27, 1944. The rest of Fuller's 41st Division followed. About 12,000 men were landed on the first day, with a number of tanks and field artillery. An M4 Sherman comes ashore in the bottom picture. Kuzumi let the Americans land in peace. His men were dug into the cliffs and caves overlooking Fuller's goal 9 miles from the landing beach: Mokmer Airdrome.

Adm. Soemu Toyoda inherited command of the Japanese combined fleet with the death of Adm. Mineichi Koga in March 1944. Based at the fleet anchorage in Davao, Philippines, Toyoda planned to intervene in the invasion of Biak. Operation KON envisioned reinforcements and a naval engagement for Biak. Code breakers again deciphered Japanese plans, and Kenney's airmen and Kinkaid's 7th Fleet held off two Japanese naval thrusts at Biak in June. Admiral Toyoda was ready to throw in Japan's super battleships *Musashi* and *Yamato* when Adm. Ray Spruance's U.S. 5th Fleet hit Saipan in the Marianas Islands.

The U.S. Navy invaded the Marianas Islands at Saipan on June 15. Marines met brutal resistance on not only Saipan but also Guam and Tinian. The invasion also brought out the Japanese fleet for a decisive naval engagement. Admiral Spruance's carrier force under Vice Adm. Marc A. Mitscher destroyed Japanese naval air power for good. The Biak and Marianas campaigns show how the divided command in the Pacific worked to keep the Japanese off balance. If the U.S. Navy had not hit the Marianas, the full weight of Japan's navy would have fallen on MacArthur at Biak.

MacArthur announced victory on June 3, but didn't have the airfields on Biak to support the invasion of the Marianas Islands. General Krueger began to feel pressure from MacArthur, and he in turn weighed on Major General Fuller (both seen here in 1944). Krueger sent in Eichelberger on June 15 to clear up the situation. Fuller knew what had happened to Harding when Eichelberger arrived in Papua, so he knew it was over. Jens Doe took over the 41st, and Mokmer Airdrome was secured on June 28, but fighting on Biak continued until August.

With Biak's situation still in flux, MacArthur looked for other airfields. Noemfoor was a 15-mile-long, 12-mile-wide island west of Biak. There were about 1,750 Japanese on the island, but taking Kamiri Airfield would give air cover throughout western New Guinea. After the landing of the 158th RCT, the 503rd Parachute Infantry made its second jump of the war on July 2. They dropped from only 400 feet and suffered more casualties in the jump than in the campaign for the island.

With the invasion of Noemfoor, Krueger had three battles going on at once. The 20th Infantry Regiment was engaged at Lone Tree Hill near Sarmi, and Doe's 41st Division was eliminating resistance on Biak. It was the troops of Lieutenant General Adachi's bypassed army, however, that were on Krueger's mind. The 32nd Division and 112th RCT awaited them at Aitape, but Adachi's assault on July 10 put the Americans on their heels. Attacking on many fronts, Adachi lost 10,000 before his forces were crushed at the end of July. In the image above, men of the 127th Infantry, 32nd Division, move to the front at Aitape.

In a little over three months, MacArthur's forces advanced 800 miles. They had to clear out a determined enemy, but they suffered only a fraction of the casualties that Nimitz's forces were taking in the Marianas Islands. MacArthur felt he was proving that the New Guinea–Philippines axis was the way to beat Japan. Behind the battle fronts, however, strategy still concentrated on a Central Pacific drive to Formosa; it was a future Douglas MacArthur could not live with.

In late July MacArthur received a radio message from General Marshall to report to Pearl Harbor. MacArthur flew out of Brisbane on July 26 and was met at Pearl Harbor by Admiral Nimitz, who informed him that President Roosevelt was arriving on the heavy cruiser USS *Baltimore*. MacArthur had a tumultuous welcome at the docks and greeted the president while posing for pictures. There were hundreds of images taken, but in the photo above MacArthur, Roosevelt, and Nimitz seem lost in their own thoughts.

MacArthur and Roosevelt enjoy a laugh on the USS *Baltimore*. MacArthur had not seen Roosevelt in seven years and was shocked at his condition, believing he would not live much longer. Roosevelt, despite all of MacArthur's political machinations in the past year, played the role of old friend and neutral agent in the strategic arguments presented by the Army and Navy.

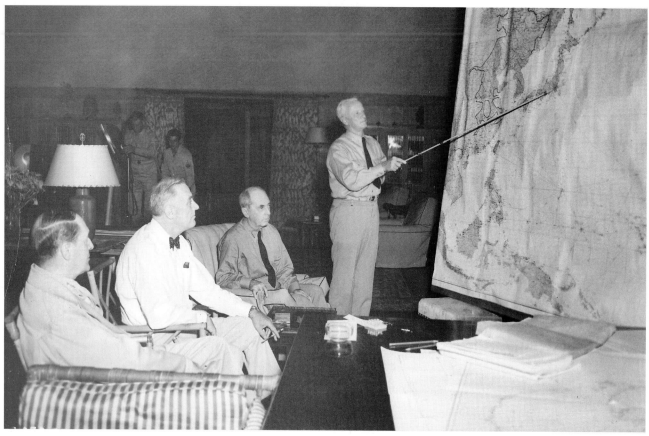

The conference was held at the Honolulu home of wealthy businessman Chris Holmes. Shown at the map, Admiral Nimitz presents Admiral King's and the Navy's plan for a drive on Formosa to MacArthur, Roosevelt, and Roosevelt's military advisor, Adm. William D. Leahy. Landing on Formosa would bypass Japanese forces in Luzon and strangle Japan by cutting the sea lanes to the Dutch East Indies. The Navy also believed the U.S. Fourteenth Air Force in China could fly support for the invasion.

MacArthur then had his turn at the map. All the goals of a Formosa drive could be accomplished at less cost by taking the Philippines. MacArthur had Philippine guerrillas ready to strike on all the islands. Everyone on Formosa was a hostile. The plan for hitting Mindanao in October, Leyte in December, and Luzon in April 1945 required less shipping than a drive on Formosa. After his presentation, MacArthur met alone with President Roosevelt and stressed the U.S. would lose face in Asia forever if the moral obligation to liberate the islands was not fulfilled.

After their private meeting, MacArthur said he was returning to Australia, but Roosevelt asked him to make another tour around in the car with him. No decision was made at Pearl Harbor; the subject was still up for discussion and debate. Eventually it came down to circumstances and opportunity as to what course of strategy would follow, but MacArthur believed he had won Roosevelt over to his argument for a return to the Philippines.

Shortly after MacArthur's return to the Southwest Pacific Area, 7,300 men of Maj. Gen. Franklin Sibert's 6th Division moved into Sansapoor in another bloodless invasion, bypassing thousands of Japanese troops at Manokwari. The move neutralized the Vogelkop Peninsula, grabbed two more airfields to support the next move to the Halmaheras, and ended the two-year drive across New Guinea.

The Halmahera Island group was the final stepping stone to the Philippine island of Mindanao. Air bases there could cover moves to the Palaus as well as the Philippines. Central Bureau's code breakers again staved off disaster, pinpointing 30,000 Japanese troops on Halmahera Island. On September 15, therefore, Admiral Barbey's VII Amphibious Force landed Maj. Gen. John C. Person's 31st Infantry Division on the lightly defended island of Morotai. The Pitoe landing area (above) was a scene of activity on the morning of the invasion.

At 10:15 AM MacArthur went ashore to visit the troops with "Uncle Dan" Barbey. The two are shown here on Morotai with their pants soaked to the waist; they had to wade ashore. XI Corps commander Maj. Gen. Charles Hall stands to the rear of MacArthur. MacArthur told Barbey that Halsey's 3rd Fleet had hit the Philippines with air strikes, getting no response. Meeting in Quebec, the Combined Chiefs wanted to know if MacArthur could immediately put together an invasion of Leyte Island, Philippines.

MacArthur poses with men of the 31st Infantry Division on the beach at Morotai. There were many reasons MacArthur was given the opportunity to return to the Philippines. His resolve and will to return was made a reality by the capabilities of men like Kenney, Krueger, Kinkaid, Barbey, Eichelberger, and hundreds of junior officers that came together as a team. The main reason, however, were the men standing next to him. American, Australian, and New Zealander boys bore the brunt of his drive to return to the Philippines and delivered him to the islands' doorstep.

MacArthur waves to the beach as the landing craft prepares to return him to the USS *Nashville*. Colonel Lehrbas, the general's aide, stands looking on. Lehrbas said that MacArthur looked in the direction of the Philippines and said, "They are waiting for me there."

When the radio message came to headquarters at Hollandia asking about the feasibility of the landing at Leyte, MacArthur was on the USS *Nashville* observing radio silence. He could receive the message but not respond. Sutherland made the decision for MacArthur and answered in the affirmative. The episode was not forgotten.

MacArthur sits on his B-17 command plane *Bataan* in 1944. His drive to Morotai brought RENO IV operations to an end. In five months, SWPA forces advanced over 1,400 miles, leaving over 25,000 Japanese dead and tens of thousands bypassed and "dying on the vine," as MacArthur would say. Code-breaking intelligence allowed him to bypass the enemy and avoid high casualty rates. The same would not be true in the Philippines.

MacArthur is seen in his leather jacket on his last day in Australia. On October 14, 1944, he left Brisbane for Hollandia to board the USS *Nashville* for the Leyte invasion. He now had the Sixth and Eighth Armies under Krueger and Eichelberger to move into the Philippines. Over 200,000 men of Gen. Tomoyuki Yamashita's Fourteenth Area Army were waiting, but so was a population primed for liberation and a guerrilla resistance movement MacArthur had been fostering since his arrival in Australia in 1942.

Lt. Col. Charles Hedges (standing center) went into the jungles of Mindanao upon word of the surrender in May 1942. He led the Lanao Maranao force of Muslim fighters (above) for Col. Wendell Fertig's 10th Military District guerrilla command. Disparate guerrilla groups rose against the Japanese occupation spontaneously throughout the islands in September–October 1942. Radio contact was established, and MacArthur approved the insertion of an intelligence party by U.S. Navy submarine into the island of Negros in November 1942. For the next two years, submarines inserted men and materiel into the islands and established a network of radio stations under recognized leaders organized under the prewar military district system. The photo above shows the men holding brand-new Browning automatic rifles, brought to the islands by the submarines.

Col. Courtney Whitney commanded MacArthur's Philippine Regional Section, coordinating, organizing, and supplying the guerrillas in the Philippines. A prewar lawyer in the Philippines, Whitney was a man of connections and capability selected for the job by Lieutenant General Sutherland.

MacArthur's top agents in the Philippines were Navy commander Charles "Chick" Parsons and Lt. Col. Charles Smith. Parsons was captured by the Japanese in Manila but returned to the United States on a diplomatic exchange early in the war. Smith, a mining engineer, sailed a boat from Mindanao to Darwin, Australia, in December 1942. MacArthur had them inserted by submarine into Mindanao in early 1943. They spent months setting up coast-watching stations and scouting the situation throughout the Philippines. It was the first of many trips for both men. Their work prompted the U.S. Navy to support the guerrilla movement.

The U.S. Navy was reluctant to waste submarines on supply missions, but the coast-watching stations established in Mindanao produced great results for the Navy's campaign against Japanese shipping. The Navy gave two of its largest submarines, the USS *Narwhal* (above) and the USS *Nautilus*, to the guerrilla program. The boats served on multiple missions, taking in tons of supplies, agents, and propaganda materials emblazoned with the statement "I Shall Return."

The Leyte Gulf invasion fleet is seen gathering in Humboldt Bay, Hollandia, prior to departure for Leyte. Kinkaid created three task forces with 700 ships. Admiral Nimitz loaned Rear Adm. Theodore Wilkinson's III Amphibious Corps, and it became Task Force 79. Wilkinson's target was southern Leyte to land the XXIV Corps, another loan from Nimitz. Kinkaid held Task Force 77 with the fleet's firepower, and Barbey's Task Force 78 would land the X Corps in the north. Admiral Halsey's 3rd Fleet provided carrier support for the operation.

General Krueger and Admiral Kinkaid look at a map of Leyte. As in all landings in SWPA, the naval amphibious commander held control until the force was landed, and then the army commander took over. Krueger had 200,000 men in Sixth Army and was going ashore with two corps, four divisions abreast of each other. Sibert's X Corps landed north around Palo and the capitol at Tacloban, and Lt. Gen. John Hodge's XXIV Corps landed 40 miles to the south around Dulag.

An aerial shot of the Leyte beachhead shows the massive size of the operation. Japanese Lt. Gen. Shiro Makino's 16th Division of 20,000 men was stationed on Leyte on the morning of October 20. In the north, the 1st Cavalry met little resistance, but the 24th Infantry Division engaged Japanese just off the beach. At Dulag to the south, the pre-invasion bombardment drove off any defenders, but the 7th and 96th Divisions of the XXIV Corps met solid resistance inland.

In two and a half years, MacArthur's forces had fought their way back to the Philippines. Aboard his landing craft to share the moment of redemption are, left to right: Lieutenant General Kenney, Lieutenant General Sutherland, President of the Philippines Sergio Osmeña, Colonel Lehrbas, MacArthur, Colonel Egeberg, and Brig. Gen. Carlos Romulo.

MacArthur fulfills his pledge to return. President Osmeña, Lieutenant General Kenney (behind Whitney), Colonel Whitney, Brig. Gen. Carlos Romulo, MacArthur, Lieutenant General Sutherland, CBS newsman Bill Dunn, and Sgt. Francisco Salveron come ashore at Palo, Leyte. This is probably the most iconic image of Douglas MacArthur, showing the general with a .38 revolver in his back pocket.

On the beach at Palo, MacArthur delivers his "I Have Returned" speech in a mobile transmitting unit created by the Signal Corps. The unit transmitted the speech to the USS *Nashville*, which broadcast it to all the guerrilla radio stations within range. MacArthur called on his guerrillas to "rise and strike." MacArthur recorded the speech in Australia before the landing, and it was broadcast from a communications ship offshore to an even broader audience. Osmeña stands behind MacArthur waiting to give his speech.

On October 23 MacArthur held a ceremony on the steps of the Tacloban capitol building, restoring civil government to the Philippines. During the ceremony, he recognized Col. Ruperto Kangleon, the 7th Military District commander of the guerrillas of Leyte. He decorated Kangleon with the Distinguished Service Cross. Kangleon became governor of Leyte and eventually the Philippine secretary of defense.

Sho 1 was the Japanese naval plan to counter an American invasion of the Philippines. Japan had lost most of its carrier planes and pilots against the U.S. Navy at the Marianas, so Vice Adm. Jisaburo Ozawa's main carrier force deployed with a few airplanes to decoy Admiral Halsey's fleet away from the landing force. When the bait was taken, Vice Adm. Takeo Kurita's and Vice Adm. Shoji Nishimura's fleets of battleships and cruisers would attack the helpless invasion fleet of transports. Sho 1 precipitated the largest naval battle in human history. Kurita's and Nishimura's fleets were both spotted in their advance to the islands; 1st Striking Force took a beating from submarines and carrier planes. The *Mushashi*, one of the largest battleships ever built, was sunk. Nishimura's fleet came through the Surigao Straits on the night of October 24–25 and found Rear Adm. Jesse Ollendorf's battle line of obsolete battleships performing the classic naval move of "crossing the T." In the photo of the Battle of the Surigao Straits above, the USS *West Virginia* fires on Nishimura's ships.

Ozawa's fleet was sighted, and Halsey took his 3rd Fleet north. Miscommunication between fleet commanders Halsey and Kinkaid left the San Bernardino Strait unguarded. Though Kurita had been hammered the previous day, on October 25 he continued into Leyte Gulf. In perhaps the greatest episode in American naval history, a handful of destroyers and jeep-carriers held off Kurita's fleet by attacking against all odds. On the verge of victory, Kurita retreated. Later in the day, a *kamikaze* airplane hit the jeep-carrier USS *St. Lo* (right). The Japanese were introducing a new weapon: the suicide bomber.

Speed was impossible on Leyte. The rains set in and mud ruled. It became impossible to get airstrips to handle even the light fighter planes or move heavy equipment around (above). The XXIV Corps tried to move inland and around the south of Leyte while the I Corps moved around the north coast and into the Carigara Mountains, but Japanese reinforcements were arriving by the thousands.

General Yamashita felt the main battle should be on Luzon, but he was ordered to make every effort to support Makino on Leyte. The 1st Division, veterans of China, was sent in along with the 30th, 102nd, and 26th Divisions through the backdoor port of Ormoc. Over 55,000 Japanese made it into Leyte. Even when Kenney's pilots could fly interdiction, the Japanese still made it. In the image above, a B-25 medium bomber flies over a Japanese reinforcement ship in Ormoc Bay.

It was the amphibious landing at Ormoc by the 77th "Liberty" Division (left) that spelled doom for the Japanese defenders of Leyte. Coming ashore on December 7, the 77th Division cut off the Japanese from their port of reinforcement and linked with forces from the X and XXIV Corps. Control of Leyte passed into American hands, but the island was jungle, swamps, and mountains, and it took many months to hunt down the defenders. Of the 60,000 Japanese who fought on Leyte, only 400 surrendered.

Three weeks before Leyte, the Joint Chiefs of Staff decided that the drive to Japan would go through Luzon. Now that Leyte was under control, MacArthur could make the jump to Luzon, but as always he needed to advance land-based air power to cover the invasion. The island of Mindoro fit the need, so on December 15 an amphibious force landed the 19th RCT and the 503rd Parachute Infantry. While accompanying the task force, the USS *Nashville* was hit by a *kamikaze*. Bodies can be seen laying on the deck.

*Kamikazes* hit a number of ships during the Mindoro invasion. In this image an LST loaded with trucks, equipment, and supplies burns furiously after being struck. Despite the attacks, the force was landed and fighter squadrons were soon operating off Mindoro's airstrips. Mindoro became a hub of air and naval traffic throughout the campaign to retake the islands.

MacArthur is shown with his staff at Christmas dinner in Tacloban. The staff looks relaxed, even playful. Organized resistance on Leyte was over. Eichelberger's Eighth Army was taking over from Krueger's Sixth Army, and the jump to Luzon was on the horizon. MacArthur and his chief of staff, Richard Sutherland, look detached and distracted. Their relationship was over. MacArthur actually placed Sutherland under house arrest on Leyte for violating orders.

With the USS *Nashville* out of action, MacArthur took her sister ship, the USS *Boise,* for the journey to Lingayen Gulf and the invasion of Luzon. Promoted to General of the Army on December 16, 1944, MacArthur wears the new insignia of a five-star general. Lingayen was chosen as the only site where Krueger could get four divisions ashore at the same time on January 9, 1945. Throughout the passage in waters to the west of Luzon, *kamikaze* aircraft plagued the convoy.

A Sherman tank comes ashore from the LST that carried it to Luzon. The landing of the 6th, 43rd, 37th, and 40th Divisions was unopposed. Yamashita created Shimbu Group with 80,000 men under Lt. Shizuo Yokoyama and placed them in the mountains east of Manila. Kembu Group under Maj. Gen. Rikichi Tsukada, with 30,000 men, was sent to the Clark Field and Bataan area, and the Shobu Group of 152,000, also under his control, pulled back to the mountain groups in northern Luzon. Yamashita knew defeat was inevitable but planned on tying up U.S. forces for as long as possible.

Once the Sixth Army landed, MacArthur pushed Krueger relentlessly to drive on south to Manila. The army needed the port facilities for resupply. Krueger was worried about Shobu Group on his flank and moved with caution. MacArthur was always at the front, urging the men on. In the image at left, the only people not taking cover are MacArthur, his party, and the stretcher-bearers. MacArthur won his third Distinguished Service Cross in action near San Manuel at the front during a firefight.

MacArthur shakes hands with Maj. Gen. Robert Beightler, who served with MacArthur in the Rainbow Division in the First World War. Now he commanded the 37th "Buckeye" Division of National Guardsmen from Ohio. While I Corps monitored Yamashita to the north, XIV Corps drove on Manila. MacArthur rode Beightler too, remarking, "I noticed a lack of drive in your division today."

While the XIV Corps moved south, the XI Corps landed on western Luzon near Subic Bay on January 29. The XI Corps' 38th Division was detailed to push east over the Zig Zag Pass and meet the XIV Corps. Here, men drop a phosphorous grenade into a Japanese-held dugout. This was the pattern that had to be followed to rout out an army that would never surrender.

Two regiments of the Eighth Army's 11th Airborne Division were put ashore at Nasugbu, 45 miles southwest of Manila, on January 31. The 11th moved inland to where its 511th Parachute Regiment parachuted on Tagaytay Ridge overlooking Manila, then advanced on Manila from the south, where the Japanese held a network of defenses at Fort McKinley and Nichols Field. Kenney wanted to fly the 11th right into Nichols Field, but Eichelberger would not even consider it.

On December 14 the Japanese commander of the prisoner of war camp at Puerto Princesa, Palawan Island, thought he was about to be invaded. He had 150 American prisoners of war, veterans of Bataan and Corregidor, herded into trenches, doused in gasoline, and then lit on fire. Those who tried to climb out were machine-gunned. Their remains are seen in the image here. A handful of prisoners escaped the horror and were found by guerrillas. They were put in contact with MacArthur's headquarters.

Col. Robert Lapham was in the 45th Philippine Scouts on Bataan. Sent on a mission with Maj. Claude Thorpe in 1942 to set up a radio unit overlooking Clark Field, he was hunted but never caught after the surrender. Lapham built an organization of guerrillas in central Luzon. When Sixth Army landed, he related there were American prisoners of war at Cabanatuan Prison Camp in between Lingayen Gulf and Manila. After what happened at Palawan, MacArthur ordered Krueger to put together a rescue mission.

Krueger picked a handful of his ALAMO Scouts, specially trained jungle fighters and reconnaissance men, to move out with the 6th Ranger Battalion under Lt. Col. Henry Mucci. They marched overland and rescued the prisoners on the evening of January 30, while a detachment of Lapham's guerrillas under Capt. Juan Pajota held off Japanese reinforcements. Pajota's men (right) fought professionally to fulfill their mission, and MacArthur awarded all of them the Bronze Star.

Of the thousands of Americans from USAFFE that went into captivity, these 500 men liberated at Cabanatuan were some of the few left in the Philippines. All the rest were taken to Japan on "hell ships" of misery and death. The Filipinos were let go months after surrender. They were dying by the thousands, beyond what the Japanese could stomach. MacArthur visited the men from Cabanatuan at their rest center in Guimba and had them tell him all the stories of depravation and cruelty.

MacArthur is seen in the Fort Stotsenberg area of Luzon with his military secretary, Brig. Gen. Bonner F. Fellers. They are with 37th Infantry Division men watching the shelling of Clark Field. MacArthur was pushing Krueger to take Clark, but Krueger waited until his reserves landed at Lingayen on January 26. Two days later the 37th took Stotsenberg, but Tsukada's Kembu Group was defending the hills next to Clark and a major fight erupted.

MacArthur arrives in Manila at Santo Tomas Internment Camp on February 7 with his corps and divisional commanders of the drive on Manila: I Corps commander Maj. Gen. Innis P. Swift, Beightler, and 1st Cavalry Division commanders Brig. Gen. William C. Chase and Maj. Gen. Verne D. Mudge. MacArthur told Mudge to race to Manila, free the internees at Santo Tomas, and capture Malacanan Palace. *LIFE* magazine photographer Carl Mydans is in the foreground.

MacArthur is swamped by the internees in front of the main building at Santo Tomes Internment Camp. For three and a half years it was home to as many as 5,000 Allied civilians caught when the Philippines were surrendered. They were on the verge of starvation, and for all MacArthur knew, execution, when the 1st Cavalry and 44th Tank Battalion broke down the gates on February 3, 1945.

Almost serendipitously the 37th Division came across the inhabitants of Bilibid Prison in northern Manila. Five hundred civilian internees from Baguio had been brought there just before Christmas, and 800 survivors of Bataan–Corregidor were living there as well. On February 7, 1945, the same day MacArthur visited Santo Tomas, he went to Bilibid. He called many prisoners he knew by name and apologized for the long time it took to get back.

A raging inferno swept through areas of Manila as fires were intentionally set by the Japanese and the sympathetic Filipino organization Makapili. There was nowhere to run for the Filipinos.

Most of Manila is devastated, and a fire from the area north of the Manila Hotel blackens the sky. Americans closed in on the city from three sides. The 37th and 1st Cavalry came in north of the Pasig River, and the 11th Airborne came from the south. Unlike MacArthur, who declared an open city in 1941 to preserve Manila, Rear Adm. Sanji Iwabuchi and 16,000 Japanese marines and sailors were there to fight to the death and teach the Americans a lesson: This is what to expect in Japan.

Most of the area north of the Pasig River was cleared by February 9, but it was south of the river that the Japanese were concentrating their forces. That was where all the huge, reinforced concrete government buildings were located. The 129th regiment crossed the Pasig River on February 23 to begin the assault on the old Spanish walled city of Intramuros.

MacArthur walks through his old penthouse apartment at the Manila Hotel, now nothing more than rubble and ash. The Japanese used it as a command post, and a battle for its possession erupted before the general's eyes. All of his lifelong possessions were destroyed. His thousands of books, First World War memorabilia, and all of his father's Civil War artifacts were consumed in the destruction. His father's Medal of Honor has never been recovered.

The difference war can make. The stark contrast between the two images of the Manila Post Office is staggering. The image at right shows the building and the city before the war. The picture on the following page shows the aftermath of the battle. Iwabuchi's decision to fight in the city led to Manila's destruction. In Europe it was thought that Warsaw was the most devastated city. Manila was called the "Warsaw of the Pacific."

Flanked by President Sergio Osmeña, MacArthur restores the Philippine government in Manila. The ceremony took place on February 27 at Malacañang Presidential Palace on the banks of the Pasig River. During the speech MacArthur was overcome with emotion and had tears streaming down his face as he finished. The Manila he knew—the Manila everyone knew—was gone. From left to right in the rear are Colonel Lehrbas, Colonel Egeberg, Lt. Col. Andres Soriano, and Brig. Gen. Basilio Valdes.

All the scuttled Japanese ships in Manila Harbor had to be emptied of Japanese snipers before they could be cleared out of the waters.

The jails of the Japanese Kempeitai secret police at Fort Santiago are filled with executed Filipinos. They were but a few of the 100,000 civilians massacred during the atrocity-filled battle for Manila.

The need to secure the port facilities in Manila made the seizure of Corregidor, blocking Manila Bay, a necessity. In a joint drive to seize southern Bataan and Corregidor, the 38th Division and the 503rd Parachute Infantry came together to storm both areas. First, the 38th Division landed on south Bataan, and then two days later, on February 16, the 503rd jumped on Corregidor. In the photo above, parachutes of the 503rd litter the parade ground in front of Topside Barracks, now nothing more than a shell.

The 34th Infantry Regiment lands on the south beach of Bottomside, Corregidor. Thousands of Japanese fought to the death on Corregidor before the 503rd and 34th could claim it was over. The pattern was so familiar now: They all fought to the death, many dying in mass suicides in the tunnels of Corregidor. The last such suicide ended the fighting with a giant explosion on February 26.

On March 2 the Bataan Gang, all the men who were removed with MacArthur by PT boat in March 1942, were reunited on Corregidor. Four were missing. The air officer, Brig. Gen. Harold George, was decapitated by an errant propeller at an Australian airbase in 1942. Paul Rogers, Sutherland's staff sergeant, got lost before the picture was taken. Col. Harold Wilson and Dr. Morhouse were no longer with the command. Left to right are Diller, Maj. Gen. Charles Stivers, Willoughby, Akin, Sutherland, MacArthur, Marshall, Casey, Huff, Marquat, and Capt. Joseph McMicking.

At the old Spanish flagpole of Fort Mills, the Stars and Stripes are raised over Corregidor once again. MacArthur said, "Hoist the colors and let no enemy ever haul them down again." It was a moment of great triumph and a spectacular scene shared by the men of the 503rd and 34th.

A mortar team of the 127th Infantry, 32nd Division, fires at Japanese on the Villa Verde Trail in March 1945. Now that Manila and Manila Bay were in the hands of the Americans, General Krueger was able to concentrate on Yamashita and the Shobu Group in northern Luzon. He moved toward Baguio with the 33rd Division covering the left flank, the 32nd in the middle on the Villa Verde Trail, and the 25th holding the right. The fighting was grueling, and many blamed MacArthur for not supplying more men to the job.

An M4 Sherman tank passes the Baguio Cathedral on April 27, 1945. Once the situation cleared up in Manila, the 37th Division was brought to the northern front and, together with the 33rd Division, drove into Baguio. Yamashita had already evacuated to the north and the high mountain region of the Cordillera. Yamashita and the Shobu Group held out until the end of the war, only surrendering at the order of Emperor Hirohito.

MacArthur had Krueger's Sixth Army working overtime with not only the drive in the north, but also offensives east and south of Manila. Here, a 2½-ton, 6 x 6 truck of the 1st Cavalry Division's "Flying Column" is enthusiastically welcomed in the Batangas area of southern Luzon. In the photo at left, men of the 38th and 43rd Infantry Divisions were having a rougher time of it trying to wrest the dams holding Manila's water supply away from Yokoyama's Shimbu Group. These men of the 149th Infantry train their .30-caliber machine gun on their enemy in the Marakina Watershed.

MacArthur's directives from the Joint Chiefs of Staff said nothing about the Visayan and Southern Islands of the archipelago, but he sent Eichelberger's Eighth Army on a mission to secure the southern passage. The campaign placed Eighth Army divisions on Palawan, Mindanao, Cebu, Negros, Panay, and Bohol. In the photo above, men of the 41st Division offload from Landing Ship, Mediums (LSM) on Mindanao's Zamboanga Peninsula in March 1945 to secure an airbase to cover future operations.

In the Cebu invasion, the Americal Division, the only U.S. division without a number, got held up on the beach for over an hour by a Japanese minefield. It was a disaster, but the Japanese didn't respond, though there were 13,000 on the island. Here, men of the Americal Division enter Cebu City on the back of an M7 Priest. The Priest carried a 105mm howitzer and saw widespread use in the Philippine campaign. The Japanese held out to the end on Cebu. When the surrender came, over 8,500 laid down their arms.

While MacArthur's forces secured the Philippines, Nimitz's forces invaded the island of Iwo Jima in the Bonins Islands in February 1945 (above). Once Iwo Jima was taken, Okinawa in the Ryukyu Islands was the final stepping stone to Japan. The last great battle of the Pacific War was perhaps the worst. The use of *kamikazes* reached its peak, and Japanese determination to resist turned Okinawa into a cauldron of death. The next step was obvious: the home islands of Japan.

Strategy was now focused on the invasion of Japan. The Joint Chiefs wanted MacArthur to move his headquarters to Guam for better contact with Admiral Nimitz and his staff. MacArthur refused. Nor would MacArthur deal with Nimitz's staff, so the admiral journeyed to Manila on May 15, 1945. As at Brisbane, he found that MacArthur in person was much different from the exacting and exacerbating character that came across in radio message traffic. Cordial and agreeable, MacArthur had Nimitz stay at his house, and they worked out all the problems their staffs were having trouble putting together.

MacArthur boarded the USS *Boise* on June 3 to witness the Australian invasions in Borneo. He also visited units and commanders on the islands of Mindoro, Mindanao, Cebu, Negros, Panay, and Palawan. He went ashore with the Australians in Borneo and on the way back to Manila stopped at Jolo Island. In the photo above, the sixty-five-year-old MacArthur looks trim and fit, but tired, with Gov. Arolas Tulawie of Jolo, Lieutenant General Eichelberger, and Col. William J. Moroney of the 41st Division.

MacArthur and General Kenney
have their ears plugged as they
watch the pre-invasion bombardment of Balikpapan from the deck
of the light cruiser USS *Cleveland*.
Unknown to both of them, the July
1 assault was the last major amphibious operation of the Second World
War. In the background is Brig.
Gen. Courtney Whitney, former
head of guerrilla operations in the
Philippines and the man becoming
MacArthur's main confidant.

It was widely thought among Australian troops that they were being wasted on operations that really didn't matter.
Here Australian troops of the 7th Division, veterans of North Africa and the early campaigns in Papua New
Guinea, move through one of Balikpapan's oil refineries. MacArthur did have plans for the Australian victory.
He told Eichelberger he was setting up for a drive to free Java with Eighth Army in September.

By July 1945 the Japanese in all the islands of the Philippines were cut off and surrounded. MacArthur removed Sixth Army Headquarters from the campaign, and Eighth Army was given control of operations in the Philippines. Sixth Army began planning for the invasion of Japan. The war was coming to an end, but as evidenced by this photo from the drive in the Cagayan Mountains, the fighting was more brutal than ever.

Tokyo is in ruins. This photo reveals the complete devastation Japan endured before its final surrender. B-29 Superfortress bombers based in the Marianas Islands erased 66 Japanese cities and killed over 300,000 Japanese civilians. It was reported that in the firebombing raids against Tokyo the canals boiled from the heat. Though surrounded and cut off, the Japanese General Staff would not consider surrender, and American planning for the invasion of the home islands continued. MacArthur was set to oversee ground operations as head of the newly established United States Army Forces Pacific Command (USAFPAC). He would be leading the largest amphibious invasion in history, with the island of Kyushu scheduled for November 1945 and Honshu in May 1946.

MacArthur's photographer, Sgt. Gaetano Faillace of the U.S. Army Signal Corps, said this was the only picture MacArthur ever posed for. Japanese diplomats had been trying for months to get the Soviet Union, a nation they were not at war with, to broker a peace deal with the West. Stalin's declaration of war in the last week of the hostilities meant the end of Japan.

On July 26, 1945, the Allied Powers released the Potsdam Declaration to Japan. It set the terms for Japan's surrender and warned of swift destruction if the ultimatum was not accepted. Japan ignored it. On August 6 at Hiroshima and again at Nagasaki on August 9, Roosevelt's successor, President Harry S. Truman, made good on the ultimatum. The dawn of atomic warfare was unleashed. The detonation of two atomic bombs prompted Emperor Hirohito to overrule his military leaders and order surrender.

A Japanese prisoner of war in the Philippines is shown the headline of the war's end in the *Free Philippines* newspaper, August 15, 1945.

He only found out about the atomic bomb a few weeks before its detonation; he didn't know the Potsdam Declaration was to be delivered. Yet it was General MacArthur whom President Truman picked to be the Supreme Commander Allied Powers (SCAP) and accept the surrender of Japan. On August 19, 1945, a Japanese negotiating team arrived in Manila to thrash out the details of surrender and the arrival of 1 million U.S. military personnel in Japan. MacArthur and a number of onlookers watch their arrival at the shell-riddled Manila City Hall.

MacArthur is seen on the balcony of his office at USAFPAC headquarters in Manila's City Hall building. The photo was taken by Faillace just before the Supreme Commander left the Philippines for Japan. Although MacArthur suffered the worst defeat in American history in the Philippines, he was retained by people who found him difficult to deal with but who knew he had the mind to make a contribution to the cause of victory. Douglas MacArthur proved them right. Now he was about to prove he was an even abler statesman, overseeing the Occupation of Japan.

# CHAPTER 9
# OLD SOLDIERS NEVER DIE . . .

MacArthur is flanked by 11th Airborne Division commander Maj. Gen. Joseph Swing (in helmet), Major General Akin, his pilot Col. Weldon Rhodes, Sutherland, Major General Byers, and Eichelberger moments after his landing at Atsugi Airbase, Japan, on August 30. Atsugi was a former *kamikaze* base and experienced a revolt only days before MacArthur's arrival. He and his staff wore no weapons, but were surrounded by well-armed men of the 11th Airborne.

Lieutenant General Eichelberger was at Atsugi to greet MacArthur. MacArthur said to him, "Bob, this is the payoff." Eighth Army was going to be the occupation army. Sixth Army did come to Japan, but it was removed by Christmas 1945. Eichelberger stayed in Japan until 1948 and then retired, bitter that MacArthur never gave him a fourth star.

General MacArthur listens to the 11th Airborne band at Atsugi with all his accoutrements of the battlefield: his "scrambled eggs" cap, Ray-Ban sunglasses, and corncob pipe. His directive was to demilitarize and democratize Japan. Though the Allied Powers gave him wide latitude, they prescribed nearly all of his activities.

MacArthur meets Lt. Gen. Jonathan Wainwright at the Yokohama Grand Hotel. The Japanese surrender negotiation team that came to Manila divulged where all the prisoner of war camps were located. Wainwright was found in Manchuria and brought to Tokyo. MacArthur insisted he join him for the surrender ceremony on the USS *Missouri*.

On the morning of September 2, 1945, dignitaries and military officers selected by Tokyo met the representatives of the Allied Powers on the starboard deck of the USS *Missouri*, which was anchored in Tokyo Bay. It is the greatest and most benevolent moment in the history of the United States.

Douglas MacArthur signs surrender documents for the Allied Powers. MacArthur used six pens to sign the two documents of surrender: four Waterman fountain pens, one belonging to Brigadier General Whitney, and his wife Jean's orange Parker Duofold, which he uses in the picture. After the ceremony, the general retired to the *Missouri* radio room and read his speech, "Today the Guns are Silent," for broadcast in the United States.

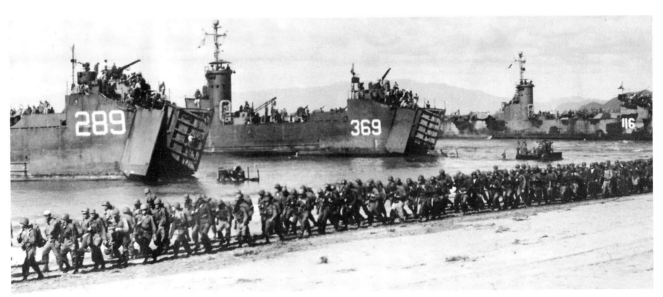

Occupation troops, all veterans of the Pacific campaigns, began arriving in Japan by the thousands. There were isolated incidents of friction and criminal activity between occupied and occupier, but generally it was a peaceful occupation.

MacArthur met with Emperor Hirohito at the U.S. Embassy a few weeks after the surrender ceremony. It was MacArthur's use of the emperor, and vice versa, that made the occupation work. Hirohito was shielded from the accusation of war crimes and urged his subjects to follow the lead of the occupiers.

For five years MacArthur ruled in Japan as the country was turned upside down with war crimes trials, purges, and social reforms. Criticized during the time, the occupation of Japan is now considered one of the great achievements of the United States. MacArthur did not return to the United States for fourteen years and by 1950 thought of himself as a sovereign power in Japan. Then, at seventy years old, he was called upon to defend South Korea from Communist North Korea.

MacArthur fought the Korean War as he had always done, with mass and concentration toward total victory. The dynamic of confronting North Korea, Communist China, and the Soviet Union in the nuclear age made Korea a delicate situation. Eventually President Truman decided General MacArthur was not in support of the administration's aim to limit and end the war without decisively defeating the enemy. He was relieved of command.

MacArthur gave his famous "Old Soldiers Never Die" speech before a joint session of Congress in Washington, D.C. on April 19, 1951. He stated his case about the Korean War, then said he would fade away and not be heard from again. Behind MacArthur are Vice President Alben Barkley (on the left) and Speaker of the House Sam Rayburn.

After the speech in Washington, the MacArthurs' reception in New York was incredible. It is still considered the largest ticker tape parade in New York history. MacArthur wasn't fading away yet. Cities across the country wanted to acclaim the victor of World War II, and even rumors of a presidential candidacy were heard. After July 1952, however, MacArthur retired to New York City with Jean and Arthur.

MacArthur made a few public appearances to give speeches in his final years, but for the most part he was reclusive. After the Bay of Pigs fiasco in Cuba, President John F. Kennedy came to see MacArthur in New York. Soon thereafter in 1961, he had MacArthur come to the White House to talk about problems in Vietnam. MacArthur arrived in the Oval Office and said, "I should have lived here."

Every year MacArthur's comrades from the days in the Southwest Pacific Area came together to celebrate the general's birthday at the Waldorf Astoria in New York City. The stag parties were a chance to reminisce about the most indelible experience of all their lives. On January 26, 1957, General MacArthur was reunited with the team that won the war in the Southwest Pacific. Krueger, Kenney, MacArthur, and Kinkaid pose for the photographer. The look on Krueger's face is classic.

Douglas MacArthur died on April 5, 1964. He lay in state in New York and then at the Capitol building in Washington before being transferred (above) to his final destination in his mother's hometown of Norfolk, Virginia. He was buried on April 11, thirteen years to the day after being relieved of command by President Truman.

Douglas MacArthur was one of the most controversial people in American history, yet he is known as the protector of Australia, the liberator of the Philippines, the conqueror and steward of Japan, and the defender of Korea. He was proud, and many thought him egotistical, but he proved himself a capable general in three wars and an able statesman during the occupation of Japan. He is the perfect example of how the power of an individual can make a difference and affect the course of world history. He is buried in the memorial that bears his name in Norfolk, Virginia, USA.

# SELECT BIBLIOGRAPHY

Barbey, Daniel. *MacArthur's Amphibious Navy: Seventh Force Amphibious Operations 1943–1945.* Annapolis: United States Naval Institute, 1969.

Bartsch, William H. *December 8, 1941: MacArthur's Pearl Harbor.* College Station: Texas A&M University Press, 2003.

Chase, William. *Front Line General.* Houston: Pacesetter, 1975.

Drea, Edward. *MacArthur's ULTRA: Codebreaking and the War against Japan, 1942–1945.* Lawrence: University Press of Kansas, 1991.

Egeberg, Roger O. *The General: MacArthur and the Man He Called 'Doc'.* New York: Hippocrene, 1983.

Eichelberger, Robert L. *Our Jungle Road to Tokyo.* New York: Viking, 1950.

Horner, David. *High Command.* Canberra: Australian War Memorial, 1982.

Huff, Sidney. *My Fifteen Years with General MacArthur.* New York: Paperback Library, 1964.

Hunt, Frazier. *The Untold Story of Douglas MacArthur.* New York: Signet, 1954.

James, D. Clayton. *Years of MacArthur: Volume II.* Boston: Houghton-Mifflin, 1975.

Krueger, Walter. *From Down Under to Nippon: The Story of Sixth Army in World War II.* Nashville: Battery Press, 1979.

Long, Gavin. *MacArthur as Military Commander.* London: B. T. Batsford, 1969.

MacArthur Memorial, Norfolk, VA, Record Group-3, Records of Southwest Pacific Area.

———, Record Group-4, Records of the United States Army Forces Pacific.

———, Record Group-49, D. Clayton James Interviews.

———, Record Group-54, George Kenney Papers.

MacArthur, Douglas. *Reminiscences.* New York: McGraw-Hill, 1964.

Mayo, Lida. *Bloody Buna.* Garden City: Doubleday, 1974.

Morison, Samuel Eliot. *New Guinea and the Marianas, March 1944–August 1944.* Boston: Little, Brown and Company, 1953.

Perrett, Geoffrey. *Old Soldiers Never Die.* New York: Random House, 1996.

*Reports of General MacArthur.* Washington: Government Printing Office, 1966.

Rogers, Paul. *MacArthur and Sutherland: The Bitter Years.* New York: Praeger, 1991.

Schaller, Michael. *Douglas MacArthur: The Far Eastern General.* New York: Oxford University Press, 1989.

Spector, Ronald H. *Eagle against the Sun: The American War with Japan.* New York: Vintage Books, 1985.

Taaffe, Steven. *MacArthur's Jungle War: The 1944 New Guinea Campaign.* Lawrence: University Press of Kansas, 1998.

Whitman, John W. *Bataan: Our Last Ditch.* New York: Hippocrene Books, 1990.

# ACKNOWLEDGMENTS

This project would not have been possible without the support of the General Douglas MacArthur Foundation. All photos are from the collections of the MacArthur Memorial Archives in Norfolk, Virginia; the National Archives in College Park, Maryland; the Naval Historical Foundation in Washington, D.C.; the Hampton Roads Naval Museum in Norfolk, Virginia; and the Air University at Maxwell Air Force Base, Alabama.